Inside the Ancie

C000182358

GREEK AND ROMAN
EDUCATION

INSIDE THE ANCIENT WORLD
General Editor: Michael Gunningham

The following titles are available in this series·

*Denotes books which are especially suited to GCSE or studies at a comparable 16+ level. The remainder may be useful at that level, but can also be used by students on more advanced courses.

Inside the Ancient World

GREEK AND ROMAN EDUCATION

Robin Barrow

BRISTOL CLASSICAL PRESS

General Editor: Michael Gunningham

Previously published in Great Britain by
Macmillan Education Ltd, 1976
Thomas Nelson and Sons Ltd, 1992

Published in 1996 by Bristol Classical Press
an imprint of
Gerald Duckworth & Co Ltd
61 Frith Street
London W1D 3JL
e-mail: inquiries@duckworth-publishers.co.uk
Website: www.ducknet.co.uk

Reprinted 2001

A catalogue record for this book is available
from the British Library

ISBN 1-85399-511-8

Printed in Great Britain by
Antony Rowe Ltd

Contents

List of Illustrations

Acknowledgements

The author and publishers wish to acknowledge the following photograph sources:

British Library pp. 22, 28, 33, 34, 35, 41, 49; Fototeca Unione, Roma p.85; Hirmer Fotoarchiv Munchen pp. 19, 38 and cover; London Museum p.79; Mansell Collection pp. 44, 46, 55, 58, 60, 64, 65, 72, 75; Musée du Louvre p. 68; Courtesy Museum of Fine Arts, Boston p. 43; National Archaeological Museum of Athens p. 16; Staatliche Museum, Berlin p. 50; Courtesy of Wadsworth Atheneum, Hartford p. 25

General Editor's Preface

To get *inside* the Ancient World is no easy task. What is easy is to idealise the Greeks and Romans, or else to endow them unconsciously with our own conventional beliefs and prejudices. The aim of this series is to illuminate selected aspects of antiquity in such a way as to encourage the reader to form his own judgement, from the inside, on the ways of life, culture and attitudes that characterised the Graeco-Roman world. Where suitable, the books draw widely on the writings (freshly translated) of ancient authors in order to convey information and to illustrate contemporary views.

The topics in the series have been chosen both for their intrinsic interest and because of their central importance for the student who wishes to see the civilisations of Greece and Rome in perspective. The close interaction of literature, art, thought and institutions reveals the Ancient World in its totality. The opportunity should thus arise for making comparisons not only within that world, between Athens and Sparta, or Athens and Rome, but also between the world of antiquity and our own.

The title 'Classical Studies' (or 'Classical Civilisation') is featuring more and more frequently in school timetables and in the prospectuses of universities. In schools, the subject is now examined at Advanced Level as well as at sixteen plus and it is chiefly for such courses that this new series has been designed. It is also intended as a helpful ancillary to the study of Latin and Greek in the sixth form and below, and many of the books will be found particularly useful by those candidates working towards the Cambridge Latin Course examination. It is hoped that some topics in the series will interest students of English and History at these levels, as well as the non-specialist reader.

The authors, who are teachers in schools or universities, have each taken an aspect of the Ancient World. They have tried not to give a romanticised picture but to portray, as vividly as possible, the Greeks and the Romans as they really were.

In this book Dr Barrow traces the pattern of changing views of education from the time of the Homeric poems to the age of St Augustine. He does not minimise the contrast between the educational practice of, for example, Sparta and Athens, but at the same time he judiciously draws our attention to the similarities and common origins of what at first sight appear very different approaches to education. In this way the book is held together by a continuous thread of development: different strands of the Homeric education find their fruition, respectively, in the educational systems of Athens and Sparta; the *paideia* of the former develops in turn and then influences the growth of early Roman education, until finally there evolves the distinctively Roman education of the imperial period.

Another unifying theme is provided by the author's concern to relate ancient ideas on education to our own. The book thus serves not only as an introduction to the history of Greek and Roman education but also as a stimulus to reflection on the nature and purpose of education itself. In addition, Robin Barrow seeks at all times to set the educational practice of a given era in the wider context of social and political issues. Ancient sources are quoted extensively and through the complaints of Tacitus, the epigrams of Martial, the stories of Plutarch and the expostulations of Protagoras a picture of classical education emerges that is vital and alive.

July 1975   MICHAEL GUNNINGHAM

Author's Note

I have adopted again the policy of translation that I introduced in my *Athenian Democracy*. In a note to the latter I wrote: 'In no place, I hope, could they (my translations) be described as inaccurate or distorted, but I have allowed myself a certain amount of freedom . . . in order that a point intended by the author may be more clearly brought across to the modern reader. . . . The intention of the original has at all times been treated as more important than the vocabulary, the spirit more important than the grammar.' Here, as there, I occasionally expand a passage in translation and, once or twice, particularly with Plutarch, conflate two different accounts of the same story from separate Lives.

9

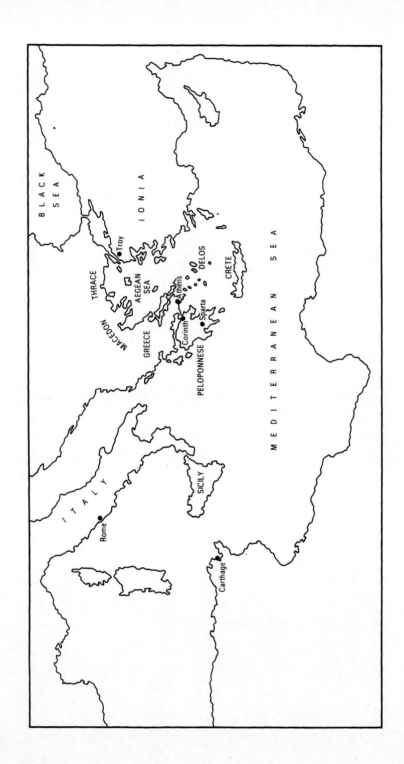

I

Introduction

'Am I not right in thinking that a good education is one that improves both the mind and the body?' asks Plato in the *Laws*. And Aristotle observed that 'the best provision for the journey towards old age is education'. On the other hand, Viscount Melbourne remarked to Queen Victoria that he could not see why people 'make all this fuss about education; none of the Pagets (a well-known, aristocratic family) can read or write, and they get on well enough.' According to Oscar Wilde, 'nothing that is worth knowing can be taught.'

So what *is* education? Why do some people value it while others regard it as a waste of time? The answer to the second question is tied up with the answer to the first. For one reason why people disagree about the value of education is that they may have different views about what education involves. Viscount Melbourne took education to mean simply teaching people to read and write, which he did not regard as particularly important. But Plato, taking it to mean the *improvement* of mind and body, obviously had to conclude that it was valuable.

Conversely, just as people's estimate of the value of education will depend on what they take education to mean, so the values of a society will to some extent dictate the nature of the education that they try to provide. The Russians, for example, because they believe in the value of a communist society, regard it as an important part of education to instil a sense of patriotism and a commitment to communism. On the other hand, the French philosopher Rousseau regarded it as quite objectionable to attempt to form children's values in any way. He valued natural behaviour above all else. He wanted to take the emphasis off books, information, traditional values and telling children how to behave. He concluded that education should consist in leaving the child to learn about the world from natural experience.

It is clear that with so many different views as to what education ought to consist of, we cannot fairly define education by simply writing down a list of things that we think people ought to learn. We cannot, for instance, say that education means 'learning maths, history and English'. What we can say is that for any society, education is that process whereby the community seeks to bring up its young to be full members of that society, sharing with others the way of life and values of that society. But the actual nature of the education provided will differ from society to society, as the way of life and values of one society differ from those of another.

It follows from this that to understand the education of a society contributes to our general understanding of that society in an important way because we are learning about the sort of things that are important to it. But here we have to be careful because it is not always possible to tell at a glance *why* a society does what it does. For example, during the second half of the last century, considerable progress was made in establishing Elementary Schools in England. In these schools the children of the poor, who had previously received no formal education, were taught to read and write. Now one might assume that this shows that there was a general recognition of the value of literacy for its own sake or a general feeling of concern for the well-being of the poor. But this was not in fact so. One of the main reasons that lay behind the spread of elementary education was the belief of the wealthier members of society that the poor would be more useful to society if they could read and write: they would be better able to do such things as take jobs as clerks and secretaries. To really understand something of the values of a society from its educational system, then, one has to see not only *what* they do in the name of education, but also *why* they do it.

In studying the education of the Greeks and Romans we may therefore hope to learn quite a lot about their respective ways of life and values. Apart from this, the story of the way in which Greek education developed, and then influenced Roman education as it too developed, has particular interest for two reasons. First, a number of similarities between the values and attitudes of the Greeks and Romans and ourselves become apparent, and we see how much we have inherited from them. And secondly, despite this, we also note fundamental dissimilarities. In particular it is noteworthy that the aim of bringing children to think for themselves rather than to assume that everything they are told by their teachers is an unquestionable truth – an aim which is now widely shared by teachers and educationalists in our society – only appears in fits and starts in the history of ancient education.

More will be said about these similarities and dissimilarities in the course of this book. But one similarity that seems to run through most societies may be noted straight away, and that is the tendency for children to dislike their education:

Oh God, oh my God, how I suffered. What torments and humiliations I experienced. I was told that because I was a mere boy I had to obey my teachers in everything. I was sent to school. I did not understand what I was taught, and was beaten for my ignorance. I never found out what use my education was supposed to be. [St Augustine, *Confessions* I 14]

These are the words of St Augustine of Hippo, one of the most miserable schoolboys the world has known. In this passage from his autobiography, *The Confessions*, he goes on to say that he was so unhappy that the only comfort he could get was to pray to God that he would not be beaten. Those prayers were the beginning of his conversion to Christianity.

St Augustine lived in the third century AD and the education that he had was the standard education provided throughout the Roman Empire. This education was derived to some extent from the system of education in Athens in the fifth century BC. That education in turn had grown out of the aristocratic education that had produced such men as the heroes of Homer's *Iliad*.

In the following pages we shall trace the development of education from Homer to St Augustine.

2

Homeric education

THE Homeric poem the *Iliad* introduces us to a world of violence and colour, a world of humour and tragedy, and, above all, a world of action. To what extent this and the other famous Homeric poem, the *Odyssey*, record actual historical events and give us an accurate picture of the beliefs and way of life of Greeks living sometime around 1200 BC is debatable. But what is not really in doubt is that the Greeks themselves later took the Homeric poems to represent a faithful picture of the way in which their ancestors had lived. In talking about Homeric education, we are therefore talking about the education which, so far as we can judge from the poems themselves, the heroes of the *Iliad* and the *Odyssey* had. Almost certainly the early Greeks did have some such education, and later Greeks certainly believed that they did.

Achilles, Agamemnon, Odysseus, Ajax. Great heroes. Great warriors. But neither they nor any of the other warriors around the walls of Troy had ever spent a day in school. Their mathematical knowledge probably stopped short at counting; it is unlikely that they could understand any language but their own; they could not read or write. By our standards they were uneducated. But not by their standards; for their view of *paideia* (education) was not the same as ours.

Peasant education

There were two social classes in the Homeric age: the noble and the peasant. The sons of the peasants were trained from an early age to do their fathers' work, and for most of them that would mean farming. The daughters learnt to weave, to make bread, and to perform the light work around the house and farm. All children grew up to accept the rules of the society without questioning them.

For example, they would quickly learn that it was necessary for them to show respect to the nobles and that it was important to remember to sacrifice to the gods. And that was all their education amounted to: learning a trade and learning the social rules.

Aristocratic education

The children of the nobles, the heroes, did not learn to farm. The noble was a member of a small ruling class and he therefore learnt to behave in a way suitable to his superior status. He had to be a courageous warrior, of course, and a good speaker in debate. He was also expected to be a skilful athlete, an accomplished musician and a loyal friend. Above all, the aristocratic noble was expected to develop a determination to do well at whatever he set his hand to. Life was one big competition in which he had to try and beat the next man in order to gain the greater glory.

Success was what mattered to a noble. And one could even be greatly honoured for being rather unscrupulous, provided that one did it well. Odysseus, for instance, was respected as being 'most cunning', because although he often cheated and lied he did so with great success.[1] Achilles, though a great warrior, was known as 'the swift-footed', not because running was more important than other things but because that was what he was most successful at. The aim of the aristocratic *paideia*, which we find referred to in the poems of Homer, was to produce a man who was a successful warrior, athlete, singer of songs and huntsman.

ATHLETICS

The Greeks were always devoted athletes. In such events as the foot-race, javelin-throwing and wrestling bouts they had an opportunity to keep fit, to enjoy themselves and to compete with each other for glory and honour.

When Odysseus landed on the island of King Alcinous of the Phaeacians, on his journey home from Troy, he had to listen to the story of the fall of Troy from the minstrel Demodocus. Naturally this upset him considerably: he had been ten years away from his wife fighting at Troy, and he had now been nearly ten more years trying

[1] See further M. A. Thorpe's *Homer* in this series.

1 *A bard or minstrel such as Demodocus*

to get home. Hearing the story of how several of his friends had met their deaths, and being reminded of how far away from home he was, he wept. (Greek heroes were not ashamed to weep when they felt like it.)

His host Alcinous sees the tears and thinks of a way to cheer up his guest. The obvious answer is an athletics contest.

Leaders and counsellors of Phaeacia, I beg your attention. We are all, I think, well pleased with this fine banquet and the familiar music of the lyre. But now let us go outside and compete in various games, so that our guest here will be able to tell everybody when he gets home that we have the champion boxer, the champion wrestler, the champion jumper, yes and the champion runner, right here in Phaeacia.

A race track is marked out in the dust of the assembly place and various events then take place, including running, wrestling, and discus-throwing. Alcinous' son Laodamas, who has just won the foot race and is therefore feeling rather full of himself, takes a look at Odysseus and seeing that he looks strong and healthy, challenges him.

Come, my dear stranger, why don't you join in the competition, assuming that you are familiar with these games? Indeed I imagine that you must be familiar with them, for there is no greater glory in life for a man than the glory he can win by his own efforts in such contests.

Odysseus replies that he is feeling rather homesick and that his mind is not on athletics contests. Laodamas thinks that this is a poor excuse and insultingly replies:

I don't believe that you're any good at athletics.

Odysseus is infuriated and after an angry word to Laodamas, he

seized an enormous discus, not even bothering to strip off his cloak first, and hurled it from his massive hand with a whistling sound. Down to the ground stooped all the spectators as the stone discus sped over their heads and far beyond all the previous markers.

Then, feeling rather more cheerful, Odysseus said,

Now if any of you have the courage, come forward and challenge me, for you have annoyed me greatly. Boxing, wrestling, running – whatever you care to mention. You will find me a dangerous opponent in any athletics contest known to man. [Homer, *Odyssey* VIII 104ff]

MUSIC

Music, as part of the aristocratic education, did not mean learning anything about harmony or the theory or history of music. In fact it always referred to songs and never to music without words. But, in the form of recitation of heroic stories to the accompaniment of the lyre, it was no less important than athletics as part of a noble's education.

They loved to hear stories of courage sung by the minstrels, as Odysseus heard Demodocus sing about Troy before the athletics contest; but they also needed to be able to play the lyre and sing if they were to be thought of as fully educated. When Achilles, perhaps the most warrior-like of all the warriors, withdrew to his tent because he thought that he had been insulted by Agamemnon,

he consoled himself by playing his clear-toned and beautifully-made lyre, which had a bridge moulded out of silver. He had taken the lyre as part of his share of the spoils when he had sacked the city of Eetion. Now he sang of the valour and glory of heroes, cheering his heavy heart. [Homer, *Iliad* IX, 184ff]

The view that an educated man ought to be familiar with a repertoire of songs, and be able to sing them while accompanying himself on the lyre, may at first sight seem rather strange to us. But there are, in fact, a number of parallels even in our own culture. Not so long ago such accomplishments as being able to play tennis or play the piano were regarded by many as essential characteristics of the educated man. And today there are some who would argue that a properly educated man should be familiar with the great works of English literature such as the plays of Shakespeare. But it should be remembered that the songs that the Homeric heroes came to know and sing had, for them, a particular relevance: for in these songs were contained stories of courage and honour and examples of great heroes, sometimes gods or demigods, sometimes mortals, which served to inspire the singer and his audience towards the Homeric ideal of bravery, honour and success.

TEACHING BY EXAMPLE

Almost as important as what the children of nobles learnt was the manner in which they learnt it. The child of a noble did not go to school for a certain number of hours each day. There were no schools. He learnt all the time. He did not learn from books – there were none – but learnt from experience. And he was not taught by a school-master; he learnt from the example of others, in particular from the example of some trusted friend of the family who undertook to bring the boy up.

Naturally the friendship between two men who were thrown together in this way could be very deep, and one of the strongest

2 *A muse playing the lyre*

reasons that a Greek hero had for conducting himself worthily was in order to bring credit, rather than shame, to his friends.

Achilles had been entrusted to the care of Phoenix by his father; and so it is that when Achilles is planning to leave the Greeks at Troy one of the most persuasive of those who try to make him stay is Phoenix.

Then the aged Phoenix spoke with tears in his eyes: 'If you are really determined to return home, glorious Achilles, and absolutely refuse to help defend our ships against the fire arrows of the Trojans because of your deep anger – then how do you imagine that I can stay here alone, without you, dear child? On the day that you, while still so young, and without any experience of war, were sent to join Agamemnon, your old father sent me to look after you. He sent me because you needed guidance in all matters, he sent me to teach you to act and to speak always in such a way as to win credit . . . As you know, I brought you up to be what you are, and many is the time in the past when you have soaked my tunic as you helplessly spluttered out your wine while sitting on my lap.'

[Homer, *Iliad* IX 434ff]

Conclusion

Homeric or aristocratic education was designed to produce individual heroes. These heroes had a lot in common: they shared the same ideals, they had the same sort of talents and they were bound together by the store of songs and legends with which they were all familiar. None the less there was no emphasis on the idea of co-operation in their education. The stress was always on the need to do better than the next man. Not surprisingly the Homeric heroes were always squabbling with each other. They could unite when they saw reason to, as they did when they followed Agamemnon to Troy. But once they were there, frequent rivalries, jealousies and feuds arose between them.

The most famous example of such a feud is that between Achilles and Agamemnon himself. The two quarrelled over which of them should take a slave girl as part of his share of the loot from a campaign. Neither of them could tolerate the idea of giving in to the other and thereby losing face. For one of them to give in to the other would involve disgrace, and so both refused to give way. This feud between Agamemnon and Achilles was one of the reasons that the Trojan war lasted so long: for most of the ten years that the Greeks were camped outside the walls of Troy Achilles was sulking in his tent, enraged at the slight he had received from Agamemnon. Without Achilles and his army the Greeks were powerless to defeat the Trojans.

To some extent our educational system, at least until recently, has shared this emphasis on the desirability of competition and the idea that it is important to strive to do better than those around one. (Although, of course, the sort of things in which competition has been encouraged have been very different.) But in other respects it is hard to see any connection between what the Homeric Greeks meant by education and what we mean by it. Their lack of knowledge about the world, particularly their lack of any kind of scientific knowledge, coupled with their tendency to explain all the features of the world with which they were familiar in religious terms, is the main reason for the difference. A great deal of time in our schools is devoted to providing skills such as reading and writing, providing information (historical, geographical, scientific or whatever), teaching children what is involved in doing such things as mathematics or chemistry, and, above all, encouraging people to see the difference between different kinds of question and then to think for themselves about the answers to them.

All this would have been meaningless to someone like Achilles. There was no great store of historical information for him to find out about – merely the vague legends of the past handed down in the songs he knew. There was no real geographical information. There was no such thing as a map of the world, and when the first maps were drawn some hundreds of years later they bore virtually no relation to what the world actually looked like. There was no such thing as science. Rain, for instance, was to be explained as a gift from the gods to make the crops grow. There was nothing for a Homeric hero to make up his own mind about, for, as far as he was concerned, the way in which he had been brought up to live and view the world was unquestionably the right way.

None the less Homeric education is of considerable importance to us, as it affects the future or Classical age of Greece in two ways: first, the emphasis on music and athletics remained. Later Greeks continued to regard musical and athletic activities as essential to an educated man. When Athens became fully democratic and, in theory, a city of freedom and equality, there was still a clear distinction between the educated gentleman, who practised such pursuits as music and athletics and regarded himself as naturally superior, and

3   A rhapsode. *A* rhapsode *was originally a composer and reciter of epic poetry. By classical times he generally confined himself to reciting the works of others, particularly the Homeric poems*

the *demos* or uneducated masses who had little time for such things and who had not been brought up to take part in such activities.

Secondly, the Homeric poems themselves, from which we have pieced together this picture of education in early Greece, later became the single most important feature of a child's education: the songs that a fifth-century Athenian learnt included, as the most loved and admired of all, the *Iliad* and the *Odyssey*. An Athenian who did not know the stories told by Homer would have been very unusual. The world of the swift Achilles and the cunning Odysseus lived on in the imagination of the later Greeks.

3
Spartan education

The Spartan *polis*

THE two most important things about the aristocratic education
were that it aimed at producing an individual hero, who would hope
to outdo his rivals, and that it worked by means of personal example.

Sparta was the first Greek *polis* (city) to drop these two ideas. In
place of the idea of personal success she put forward the idea of the
success of the *polis* or community; and in place of the idea of
entrusting the upbringing of a child to some individual she turned
to a system of education firmly organised and controlled by the *polis*.

The new educational arrangements were part of a much wider
political reorganisation supposedly carried out by a man named
Lycurgus in 750 BC. It is very difficult to be sure whether Lycurgus
actually did exist, and, if he did, whether the new arrangements were
really introduced by him, all at one time, in response to an oracle
delivered at Delphi, as the Spartans themselves later believed. The
nature of the change that took place was so radical and far-reaching
that it is difficult to believe that it could have happened suddenly
and under the inspiration of one man.

All that is certain is that a change did come about at some time
between 750 BC and 650 BC and that the new political system was
then rigidly maintained for several centuries. The most likely
explanation of the change, regardless of whether Lycurgus was
involved in it or not, is that it came about as a direct result of the
conquest of neighbouring Messenia by the Spartans. The city of
Sparta had originally consisted of five separate and unfortified
villages by the river Eurotas in the Peloponnese. By an early date in
her history Sparta had gained control of Laconia, enslaving the
original inhabitants of the area, who became known as helots. The
helots, who were Ionian Greeks, were of a different race from the
Spartans, who were Dorians and who had invaded Greece from the

north in about 1100 BC. Once conquered and enslaved, the helots were ruthlessly controlled by the Spartans. Other Dorian settlements in Laconia had also been reduced to dependence on Sparta, although these *perioeci*, as they were known, were not actually treated like slaves.

When Messenia was also conquered, by about 750 BC after a series of bloody wars, and all the inhabitants of that area had been enslaved as helots, the Spartans faced a threatening situation. They were few in number themselves and yet they had won control of half the Peloponnese, and they had to keep control of an enormous number of helots and prevent them from rising in rebellion. The problem of how to maintain the power that had been won was solved with one bold stroke.

The whole citizen body of Sparta was turned into an army, while the various trades were left to the *perioeci* and the farming was left to the helots. Communications with the outside world were cut down to a minimum. The Spartan citizen became a full-time soldier, living most of his life as a member of a communal barracks. The most important thing for Sparta was security and control over the helots. That consideration dictated the Spartan system of education.

THE SPARTAN IDEAL

The Spartan educational system was designed to produce courage and loyalty to the state. The poet Tyrtaeus expresses the ideals of patriotism and community spirit in these lines, composed to boost the morale of the citizen-soldier.

I would hardly notice a man, still less write about him, just because he happened to be a champion runner or wrestler – no, not even if he was as big and as tough as the Cyclops or as fast as the North Wind. I am not impressed by a man's good looks, his wealth or power. There's only one quality worth admiring in a man, and that's plain courage. To stand firm in the line of battle, without giving way, courageously scorning flight and putting heart into one's fellow soldiers – that is something to be proud of, something worth aiming at. A man who acts in this way is a blessing both to the people and the *polis*. [Tyrtaeus, I]

Tyrtaeus deliberately rejects the earlier heroic ideal of success for the individual in the foot-race, lyre-playing or suchlike. Now success is only worthwhile if it is success for the *polis* in some activity that

4 *A bronze statuette of a Spartan warrior*

helps the *polis*. It is the community that matters and not the individual hero. Achilles would have made a very bad Spartan.

THE LYCURGAN REFORMS

The community spirit that Tyrtaeus appeals to was deliberately created by the Lycurgan reforms. The land controlled by Sparta was divided amongst the citizens into equal shares, but these shares were to be worked by the enslaved helots. Property was also equally divided, and the only permissible form of money consisted of great iron bars so that nobody could secretly amass a fortune. Every Spartan was to be equal. Works of art were not encouraged; furniture and other household items were to be designed for usefulness and not attractiveness.

The Spartan men, between the ages of twelve and thirty, lived in communal barracks; at thirty they were allowed to marry and to visit their wives in order to sleep with them; but the barracks continued to be the centre of their life. The Spartan citizen grew up to see his duty and his own best interest served by living for the *polis* and not for himself.

Educational organisation

The organisation of Spartan education can be made to look much more difficult than it is. The Spartans themselves took the matter so seriously and organised it so carefully that for virtually every year of his life the child was known by a different title. Thus, a *propais* is a young boy, probably aged eleven; he is one year younger than a *pratopampais* and one year older than a *mikizomenos*.

These titles are not very important, however. What matters is that from the age of seven onwards the Spartan child became a member of a group in which he spent his entire waking day; and from the age of twelve he left home and lived only with the other members of his group. He never had anything that we should call a private life until he was thirty, at the earliest.

THE PAIDONOMOS

In charge of the entire city's education was the *Paidonomos* (Supervisor of Education). This was an important post filled only by a member of the highest class in the *polis*. The *Paidonomos* was helped by a staff of young men with whips, who no doubt helped to keep the children in order. Naturally the *Paidonomos* could not watch over every child personally; his job was one of general responsibility and superintendence. Therefore the children were divided into groups and placed under the immediate authority of various *eirenes* (young men of nineteen or twenty years) who were coming to the end of their own education. Probably each *eiren* would have to split his group up into still smaller units led by one of the boys in it.

SPARTAN GIRLS

Plutarch, who has left us a detailed account of the Spartan way of life in his *Life of Lycurgus*, tells us that

The Spartan girls have to wrestle, run and throw the javelin in order that when they have babies those babies should be strong and healthy, because they are born from strong and healthy mothers. Furthermore, so that women do not become too gentle or frail they are expected to walk naked in the religious processions with the young men and to dance naked as well at certain feasts. [Plutarch, *Life of Lycurgus*]

In other cities Spartan women very often became figures of fun.

Aristophanes, for instance, in his comedy *Lysistrata* introduces a Spartan girl called Lampito who is clearly a strapping great creature, the very reverse of feminine.

FIRST GIRL: Here comes Lampito now.

LYSISTRATA: Hullo there, Lampito darling. But my dear, how sweet you look, how healthy, how, how shall I put it, how tough. I do believe you could fell an ox.

LAMPITO: Begad and I could that. Naked exercise, jumping on the spot, heels kicked up behind, that's what does it.

LYSISTRATA: It does do it, doesn't it? Such beautiful bust development, darling. [Aristophanes, *Lysistrata* 76ff]

SPARTAN BABIES

When a baby was born, Plutarch tells us,

it is a rule that the father should take it before a group of the elders of his tribe. If they think that the child looks healthy, they give the order that it should be allowed to live, and they allot a share of land to it. On the other hand if they think that it looks weak or sick, they order that it should be exposed to die, on the grounds that it will help neither the baby itself nor the *polis* to live in a weak condition.

[Plutarch, *Life of Lycurgus*]

If the baby is judged to be healthy it is brought up at home until the age of seven by its mother, with the help of a nurse.

AIMS OF THE SPARTAN PAIDEIA

The Spartan children all lived together, exercising and playing together under the same rules and conditions. The older men kept a close eye on them and deliberately tried to stir up trouble amongst them to see how they all reacted. The whole aim of the education at this stage was to produce obedience. [Plutarch, *Life of Lycurgus*]

That was Plutarch's opinion. Another aim was clearly physical toughness, as Xenophon, an Athenian admirer of Sparta, points out:

The *Paidonomos* insisted that instead of wearing sandals which would soften their feet, they should harden their feet by wearing no shoes; his idea was that as a result they would be better able to scale hills and clamber down ravines. [Xenophon, *The Lacedaimonians* II 3]

After the age of twelve the children were only allowed one garment to wear throughout the year and they had to sleep out in the open, even in winter, making beds out of rushes which they cut from the river banks with their own bare hands.

And yet a third aim, no less important than physical courage, was what we may call steadfastness or mental courage. Xenophon tells us that they were fed on plain food – and very little of that. They were not discouraged from stealing, provided that they were not caught. But to be caught, since it involved failure, was a great disgrace and brought with it severe punishment.

Plutarch summed it up in this way: 'The main purpose of their education was to teach them to endure pain and to be successful soldiers and good citizens.'

WHAT DID THEY LEARN?

To be a good Spartan citizen it was not necessary to be an accomplished lyre-player, although the Spartan did have a repertoire of patriotic ballads. Apparently being a poet or musician did not count as being a good citizen; at any rate we hear of no new poets or musicians in the *polis*. The situation seems much the same in respect of athletics. The records for the great festival at Olympia, which

5   *A Spartan warrior: grim and silent*

first took place in 776 BC, reveal that for many years the Spartans produced champion athletes who won a great many victories. But then, suddenly, we cease to find any record of Spartan competitors at all. It seems that this is just one more example of Sparta withdrawing into herself. The Spartans were no longer interested in athletic competition; they were now only interested in physical exercise as a way of keeping fit.

According to one ancient writer, 'the Spartans do not approve of children learning music, writing and reading,' and, although this may be put a little strongly, we may believe Plutarch when he says that Spartan children were taught only so much reading and writing as they would need for the necessities of living.

The Spartans did attempt to widen the education of children to include such things as discussion of whether a certain type of behaviour was good or bad. But, so far as we can judge, individuality or personal opinion was not encouraged in such discussions. Clearly the idea was that all children should grow up with similar opinions and to make similar judgements: the opinions and judgements of the *polis*.

So when we ask what the Spartan children learnt, we should not have in mind a picture of a row of desks, bits of information, debate and thought. The Spartans learnt a way of living. And they learnt it by living it every minute of every day.

Conclusion

The first thing to be said about the Spartan *agoge* (system of education) is that it worked. This of course is not necessarily to praise it, since even bad things can work. But critics of Sparta sometimes ignore the fact that the Spartan education achieved what it was designed to achieve. It produced the most stable *polis* in Greece. The Spartans were courageous, loyal and proud of their way of life.

The famous story of the Spartan boy and the fox illustrates very well how strong the effect of this education might be:

On one occasion a boy stole a fox to eat and hid it under his cloak. When he was caught he let the fox tear out his guts, and died on the spot, rather than admit that he had been stealing, because of the shame of being caught – and indeed I myself [says Plutarch] can well believe it, for I have seen Spartan boys prepared to be whipped to death rather than shame themselves. [Plutarch, *Life of Lycurgus*]

Spartan education resembled the education of the Homeric heroes in that no emphasis was placed on developing children's understanding of the world. In that respect it is to be sharply distinguished from most modern educational systems. None the less there are some features of the Spartan system that have been imitated by different peoples throughout history.

The English boarding school system, for instance, although it has never perhaps been quite as ruthless or demanding as the Spartan system, has obvious points of similarity: the emphasis is on removing the child from the comparative comfort of his own home and teaching him to stand on his own two feet in relatively tough conditions. This, at any rate, has been so until fairly recently, as any reader of *Tom Brown's Schooldays* will know. At the same time boarding schools have also seen it as a major part of their task to inculcate in the young a particular style of life and code of manners suitable to a class of people who were regarded as naturally superior to many of their fellow citizens.

But the most striking feature of the Spartan system was its concern to strike out individuality and to prevent the child from coming to examine for himself the justification of the various beliefs in which he was being brought up. The Spartans learnt their code of living, but they were deliberately discouraged from questioning that code. Theirs was to accept and imitate – not to reason why. In this respect there is a striking similarity between Sparta and modern totalitarian states such as China, South Africa, Russia, and, forty years ago, Nazi Germany. Naturally, all countries, rightly or wrongly, tend to influence the young towards accepting the ideals and values of their society. But what is common to Sparta and the countries just mentioned is the attempt to go one further than this and to implant an unquestioning loyalty to the state and its values – an attempt, in other words, to suppress free thought and reasoned opposition. The defence for such an educational system would no doubt have to rely on the claim that the values inculcated in children were desirable and that such inculcation brought about cohesion between the members of society. But from the point of view of those who value democracy and the democratic ideal of free thought, the Spartan system and its modern equivalents must be regarded as objectionable; for such systems involve a denial of individuality and of the right of each person to form his own opinions as to what matters in life and what the best way to live may be.

4

Athenian education

It is not only in public life that we are so attentive to freedom. We show the same tolerance and lack of suspicion towards each other in our private lives. We don't hold it against our neighbour if he gets on with what he wants to do in his own way. [Thucydides, II 37]

These are the words of Pericles, the *strategos* (general) who effectively controlled Athens from the middle of the fifth century till his death in 429 BC. There are many similar references in other writers to Athens as a city of freedom and variety, and so it comes as no surprise to discover that Athenian education bore hardly any resemblance to the *agoge* of Sparta. It is much more like a continuation of the Homeric education.

The aim of Athenian education

The Athenian writer and teacher Isocrates, looking back on the early fifth century one hundred years later, remarks:

Our forefathers were concerned about young children. They saw that it was impossible for all of them to be educated to do the same thing, so they laid it down that each child should be brought up to take on a job suitable to his background. The children of the poorer citizens learnt farming, or buying or selling . . . while the wealthier ones had an education in which they learnt to take part in hunting, athletics and the more intellectual pursuits. [Isocrates, *Areopagiticus* 44–5]

Isocrates is obviously talking about a time at which a real education is still reserved for the gentleman or noble.

The aim of this *paideia* was to produce the *kaloskagathos*. This word literally means 'a beautiful and good man', but it was used by the Athenians as a convenient shorthand to express something like 'an honourable man, physically fit, and well-mannered'. Such a man –

the Athenian gentleman – differs slightly from the Homeric hero because, of course, times have changed and society has altered. None the less the Homeric heroes such as Achilles still represent the examples to which the Athenians look up. And, as we see from Isocrates, the Athenian gentleman is brought up to do essentially the same things as the Homeric heroes: hunting and athletics, for instance.

Isocrates does not mention *mousike* by name as an essential part of the education of a *kaloskagathos*, but we know that it was. There is a story of the *strategos* Cimon, who, when visiting a friend one evening,

was asked to sing after the meal was over. He sang – and most charmingly too, with the result that all the guests began to say how much better educated he was than his rival, the *strategos* Themistocles. For Themistocles had been in the habit of boasting that he had never learnt how to sing or play the lyre, although, he added, he knew well enough how to make a city prosperous. [Plutarch, *Life of Cimon*]

EDUCATION OF GIRLS

Socrates once asked a friend of his named Ischomachus whether he had had to teach his wife anything before she was able to take over the management of their reasonably wealthy household.

'Of course,' replied Ischomachus. 'When I married her she was not quite fifteen, so what do you imagine she knew? She had lived a very sheltered life up to then, seeing, saying and hearing practically nothing. With such an upbringing it is surely hardly surprising that when we were married she knew no more than how to weave a woollen cloak and to superintend the servants while they did the spinning.' [Xenophon, *Oeconomicus* VII 5]

We cannot be certain that this girl's lack of education is typical of Athenian girls. And it must be admitted that we know of some women who could read and write. On the other hand we know of many others who could not and we also know that the philosopher Plato, writing in the fourth century, thought that his proposal that girls should be educated along with boys would seem revolutionary to his audience. It therefore seems reasonable to conclude that in most cases Athenian girls remained at home throughout their childhood, learning little more than such household tasks as weaving and such habits as modest behaviour from their mothers.

6 *This scene shows that some Athenian girls at least were taught dancing*

Children

Weak or sickly babies might be exposed to die on the mountainsides at Athens, but it probably did not happen often, and when it did it would be decided by the parents and not the *polis*.

Small children were brought up at home by their mothers, who might have help from a nurse or one of the slave girls. Life at home seems to have been fairly easy-going compared with life for a Spartan boy. At any rate in Aristophanes' play the *Clouds*, the old farmer Strepsiades who has had to act as nurse to his son, evidently feels that his son has no right to complain:

STREPSIADES: You ungrateful brute. And to think that I brought you up with my own hands. Quick as a flash I was at guessing what your gurgles meant. No sooner had you gone 'groo' than I had a drink ready for you; 'grah' and I had a piece of bread; 'cahcah' – and, almost before you'd said it, I'd grabbed you and whisked you through the door to get on with it. [Aristophanes, *Clouds* 1341ff]

All the tricks known to parents today seem to have been known to the parents of men like Pericles and Cimon. Babies that wouldn't go

7   *A baby's bottle*

to sleep were rocked or lullabies were sung to them. The rattle was invented by a philosopher to stop children breaking things because, he said, it was impossible for the creatures to keep still for a moment. Naughty children would sometimes be frightened into good behaviour by frightening stories of bogeymen and hobgoblins who carried bad children away. And then there were the fables of Aesop, which seem as old as time to us, but which had only just been composed then.

The great variety of ingenious toys that can now be bought for children certainly were not available then, but there is no reason to suppose they were missed. Athenian children did play with hoops, balls, and swings. In fact it is rather surprising to discover just how many games that we play today were also played by Greeks, from Achilles to Alexander the Great. The tug of war, for instance, and a version of blind man's buff in which the child who was 'it' would chant, 'I shall hunt the Copper fly' and the others would reply, 'Catch it you can't but you can try'. Another favourite game was knucklebones. Alcibiades, the nephew of Pericles, was particularly fond of it:

One day when he was playing knucklebones in a narrow street, and was just about to take his throw, a wagon, loaded to the top, came along. He told the driver to stop, because his bones had fallen in front of the wagon. The driver took no notice and the other children jumped out of his way. But Alcibiades just lay down in the road and dared the driver to run over him. [Plutarch, *Life of Alcibiades*]

8 *Knucklebones*

Incidentally, although Alcibiades seems to have been a rather wilful and difficult person all his life, this story does remind us that we are dealing with Athens. It is hard to imagine such behaviour going on in Sparta where any adult was legally entitled to punish anybody else's child if it was found behaving badly.

Schools

Even as late as the fifth century the idea of entrusting a child to the care of one person who would see to its education (as Phoenix saw to the education of Achilles) had not disappeared altogether. We happen to have preserved, for instance, the verses that Theognis, a citizen of Megara at the end of the sixth century, wrote for his friend Cyrnus. The verses were full of advice – some of it pretty tedious – and it is clear that Theognis is a kind of personal tutor to Cyrnus:

Cyrnus, it is with the best of intentions towards you that I am about to pass on the wise sayings that I learnt from trusted men when I was a boy. Take my advice, Cyrnus, and do not try to win wealth or a reputation for honour by dishonest means. Do not associate with bad people; make sure that all your time is spent with respectable people. [Theognis, 26ff]

But we also know that by 500 BC at the latest (and almost certainly a hundred years before) there were schools in Greece where certain basic things like reading and writing could be learnt. The historian Herodotus records that before a battle which took place in 494 BC,

the roof of a school fell in while some children were doing their writing exercises. There were one hundred and twenty children, but only one escaped. [Herodotus, VI 27]

Most upper-class Athenian boys probably went to school by the beginning of the fifth century, although the example and friendship of slightly older boys and young men was still regarded as an important part of education. But it should not be imagined that 'school' meant one fairly big building to which several hundred boys from the neighbourhood went. The English word 'school' is derived from the Greek word *schole*; but *schole* did not come to mean anything like 'school' until late in history – originally it meant simply 'leisure' and it changed its meaning because discussion and argument were things that people did in their leisure time *and* at what we now call school. But in the fifth century the Athenians did not talk about going to the *schole*; they talked instead about going to the house of this or that teacher. And although Herodotus talked of one hundred and twenty pupils, most teachers probably had a room, perhaps hired, in which they taught ten boys or less.

The *didaskalos*

There were three kinds of *didaskalos* (teacher) at Athens. The *paidotribes* (the physical training instructor), the *kitharistes* (lyre player – and so music teacher) and the *grammatistes* (elementary schoolmaster) whose name literally means 'one who teaches letters'. These three between them were responsible for all that the Athenians thought necessary in the way of formal teaching.

For some inexplicable reason parents throughout history, while insisting that the teachers to whom they entrust their children should be well-qualified and responsible people, have had very little respect for these same teachers and have been quite happy to see them paid less money than dustmen. Athens was no exception. To be a *didaskalos* was to be more or less a nobody. The orator Demosthenes, for instance, when casting around for a really nasty insult to hurl at his enemy, Aeschines, comes up with this:

Now you – you, so stuck up, so scornful of everyone else – just compare your past life with mine. You were brought up in total poverty. You actually helped your father sweat it out in the schoolroom, grinding the soot for the ink, scrubbing down the benches, and sweeping the room. Aeschines, I suggest that you calmly – calmly, I say – compare your background with mine and then ask the jury whether they'd rather have been you or me. You were booed at – I did the booing; you taught the ABC – I was the pupil. [Demosthenes, *On the Crown* 285]

And Aeschines himself, in a passage which gives us some interesting information about schools, also shows that, by and large, teachers were not thought highly of in Athens.

In the first place consider the case of *didaskaloi*. In spite of the fact that the job of a *didaskalos* depends upon his having a good reputation – nobody would hand his son over to a known rascal – yet we can see from our laws that they are not really trusted. There is actually a law that lays down what time of day a boy is to go to school and when he is to go home. The schoolroom is not to be opened before sunrise and it must be closed before sunset – and that's because nobody trusts the schoolmaster alone with his pupils in the dark. [Aeschines, *Against Timarchus* 9]

THE PAIDAGOGOS

The boy was accompanied to the schoolroom by a *paidagogos* who carried his equipment for him and remained with him in the schoolroom throughout the lessons. But the *paidagogos* had even wider responsibility. He supervised the boy almost the entire day and his task was to watch over the behaviour of the boy and to punish him if necessary. Apart from the fact that he was with the child for so much of the day the *paidagogos* may seem similar to many modern teachers. But he was not a teacher at all. The odd truth is that this man whom parents set up to keep a permanent eye on their children was a slave. Of course the child might become very fond of his *paidagogos*, and the *paidagogos* might prove a responsible and devoted guardian as did the *paidagogos* of Medea's children. The

9   *Heracles goes to school, accompanied by his* paidagogos

father of these children, Jason, was leaving Medea to marry the princess of Corinth where they were living. Medea, a foreigner without true friends in this strange land, is losing her mind at the thought of Jason's betrayal of her and her children. But her old nurse and her children's *paidagogos* evidently feel for her and share her misery.

NURSE: What news is there now, then? Don't hide it from me.

PAIDAGOGOS: Oh it's nothing. I meant nothing.

NURSE: Don't, I beg of you, don't keep anything back from me, your fellow slave. You can trust me to keep a secret.

PAIDAGOGOS: Well I overheard – nobody realised I was listening – I overheard somebody talking near the old stone seats where that holy fountain is, and he said that Creon, the king of this land and father of this princess that my Lord Jason is about to marry – he said that Creon is going to banish Medea and her children. That's what I heard. Pray God it isn't true.

NURSE: But would Jason allow his sons to be banished like that, even if he has lost all love for their mother?

PAIDAGOGOS: A new love drives away the memory of an old love. Jason no longer cares about what happens to this house for which you and I care.

NURSE: The wretch. Oh, the wretch, Yes, he is still my master, but I curse him. His friends at any rate may freely say it: he stands exposed in evil.

PAIDAGOGÒS: Is there a man anywhere who does not sooner or later betray even his friends? Has it taken you all this time to learn that a man loves only himself? [Euripides, *Medea* 64ff]

Jason may forget and betray his children, but their *paidagogos* will not. However, the fact remains that the *paidagogos* of the Greek child was a slave and the child would know that well. It is worth reflecting upon the fact that the Athenians both accepted slavery and entrusted an important part of the care of their children to their slaves.

THE GRAMMATISTES

Parents never stop going on at their children from the day they're born. From the moment the child can understand what he's told, his nurse, his mother, his *paidagogos* and even his father nag at him, telling him that he must do this, he mustn't do that – that this is good, that is bad. All is well, provided that he does as he's told. If he has other ideas he gets beaten into shape as if he were a twisted piece of wood. After this they send him to a *didaskalos*, and they tell the *didaskalos* that the boy's manners are more important than his letters or his music. [Plato, *Protagoras* 325c]

These comments are made by Protagoras who was an important educator in the second half of the fifth century, by which time significant changes had taken place. Plato wrote a dialogue, from which the above passage comes, in which Protagoras is found discussing whether people are born as good as they will ever be or whether they can be taught goodness (*arete*); his partner in the discussion is Socrates. When Protagoras talks of the traditional education, as he does here, it is clear that he is by no means uncritical in his attitude towards it.

The child went first to the *grammatistes* when he was about seven years old. And despite what Protagoras says and regardless of what parents wanted, it is doubtful whether the *grammatistes* can have had very much effect on the character of his pupils. Unlike the *paidagogos* he was not necessarily a slave – but he might be, and he was certainly not the sort of man whom the well-born child would normally expect to feel any respect for.

The seats were stools or benches in the schoolroom. There were no tables. Writing was done on wooden tablets covered with wax which could be held on the knee. The pupil was first taught to form the letters, using a stylus and scratching in the wax; he learnt by copying the teacher. When he had made reasonable progress he was allowed to use ink and papyrus instead of the wax tablets. Then, once he was familiar with his letters, he learnt to read, which must have been quite hard since the script was continuous – in other words, there were no divisions between the words. In addition, the *grammatistes* probably taught the boys some very basic mathematics: almost certainly no more than counting and adding up, division and multiplication, which were taught on the abacus, as they still are today in many countries.

But undoubtedly the most important part of this primary education, as we should call it, and the real value of the *grammatistes'* teaching was the reading, recitation and learning of Homer's great poems, the *Iliad* and the *Odyssey*. Protagoras continues:

When the children have learnt their letters and are beginning to understand the written word as well as the spoken, they are made to learn by heart the famous poets, whose works contain sound advice and good stories, as well as praise of the heroes of old, so that the child is inspired to imitate them. [Plato, *Protagoras* 325E]

Athenian children, at least at this stage of their education, do not seem to have been expected to approach the poets as great artists nor to regard the poems as literature. The child was not supposed to concentrate on a passage and explain why it was well-written. It was taken for granted that it was well-written. The reason for reading, reciting or learning Homer was that Homer was tremendously enjoyable and that in Homer one could see how men ought to behave. Achilles had learnt from the example of Phoenix; now countless Athenian boys were learning from the example of Achilles.

Homer's poems have often been referred to as the Bible of the Greeks. They were, but not in the sense that people today sometimes understand that phrase. We are inclined to forget that the Bible used to represent a great deal more to our ancestors than a sacred book. It was a collection of wonderful tales, exciting, amazing and comic; it was a storehouse of comfort; it was full of wise sayings and stories that illustrated comforting beliefs. The things valued in the Bible were the things valued by the reader. It is in this sense, and not because they happen to contain stories about the gods, that the *Iliad* and *Odyssey* are known as the Bible of the Greeks.

THE KITHARISTES

After the *grammatistes*, according to Protagoras,

the *kitharistes* [music teacher], by using similar methods to those of the *grammatistes* when he introduces the boys to Homer, tries to teach the boys moderation and to lead them away from doing wrong. The *kitharistes* teaches the boys to play the lyre and then to sing lyric songs to their own accompaniment. In this way they become more cultured, more controlled and better balanced people, and their behaviour is all the better for it. For the truth is that the whole of one's life benefits from a calm, well-ordered personality. [Plato, *Protagoras* 326A]

It is clear from the way in which Protagoras here talks about it that being taught by the *kitharistes* did not involve anything like what we should regard as a 'music lesson'. Naturally one had to be taught to play the lyre, but it is clear that the importance of the lessons with the *kitharistes* was not that one learnt about music; it

10　*The* kitharistes *or music-teacher. The pupil (seated) is a girl: some evidence that Athenian girls were not educated only in household duties*

was that one became able to sing and play the works of the poets. The value of this to the Athenians was partly that it was regarded as one of the things that a gentleman or a well-educated man ought to be able to do; partly that the poems sung were themselves, like Homer, regarded as important educationally. But in addition the Greeks were convinced that music – the mere sound of it – could have a great effect on the mood and character of the listener. Wild music, it was thought, could create a wild kind of effect in a man; gentle music could create calm. The *kitharistes* was supposed to encourage his pupils to play moderate measures so that they grew up to approve the old maxim that was written up at Apollo's shrine in Delphi: 'Nothing in excess.'

How accurate this Greek estimate of the power of music may be is not certain. Some people today scorn it as obviously absurd. On the other hand, music has been used with some success as a calming-down influence with certain kinds of mental illness. Pop music also seems to have had very definite effects on people at certain recent pop festivals. At any rate it is important to remember that the Greeks were sure that music could produce good or bad results in people to some extent. Plato felt so strongly about this that he wrote

A new style of music is to be guarded against at all times. For whenever new styles of music are introduced they bring with them new styles of behaviour and new beliefs. [Plato, *Republic* 424C]

There is not a great deal more that can be said about the *kitharistes*, because the unfortunate truth is that Greek music is one of the subjects about which historians know least. But what we do know is that the Athenians themselves regarded the *kitharistes* and the teaching that he did as extremely important. Music lessons were supposed to do for the soul or the character of a man what gymnastics did for his body. So much so that Plato observed sharply that anyone who could not sing and dance in a choir was simply not educated.

THE PAIDOTRIBES

Finally, according to Protagoras, the boys are sent to a *paidotribes* (physical training instructor) so that their bodies shall be as fit as their minds. In other words just as the *kitharistes* and *grammatistes* between them are supposed to have developed a moderate and

11　*Scenes from a music school*

reasonable character in the boy, now the *paidotribes* is to develop a sound and healthy body.

The children start going to the *paidotribes* at about the age of twelve. He trains them in a *palaistra* (wrestling school), teaching them to box, run, wrestle – in short all the things that the Phaeacians had competed in when Odysseus was visiting them. The *palaistra* was a large unroofed square, surrounded on all sides by a colonnade and changing rooms. There were a good number in the city, some privately-owned by instructors, others publicly-owned. The public *palaistrai*, at which the adult population spent a good deal of its time, came to be quite popular meeting places. For instance Socrates says to a friend:

Last night I returned to Athens after being away for some time serving in the army, so I thought that I would go and look for some of my old

12　*The palaistra: the wrestling school of the gladiatorial barracks at Pompeii in Italy*

friends. I went down to Taureas' *palaistra* and found quite a number of people I know. [Plato, *Charmides* 153A]

A full list of the sports that children were introduced to as part of their physical education would include: running, long jump, throwing the discus, throwing the javelin, wrestling, boxing and the *pankration*. In addition a particularly popular event at the various Games festivals was the *pentathlon*, which consisted of competition in each of the first five of the events listed above. Historians are not agreed on the details of the *pentathlon*, but it seems certain that the winner of the contest had to come first in three out of the five events and that wrestling was always the final event.

Wrestling and boxing, though differing considerably from their modern equivalents, were not particularly violent: there were three rounds to a wrestling match and the object was to throw one's opponent to the ground. Boxing took place without either rounds or a ring: the competitors simply went on until one gave up from exhaustion. But in both events there were specific rules forbidding various kinds of savage blow or move. This was not so in the *pankration*, which was really just an all-out fight in which virtually anything was allowed, including kicking and biting. (Contestants were not, however, allowed to poke each other's eyes with their fingers, and the fact that the contest took place on muddy ground may have served to lessen the brutality of this particular event.)

The love of competition had in no way died out amongst the Athenians, but the *paidotribes* was not trying to produce individual champions at this or that sporting event. In accordance with the ideals of traditional Athenian education his aim was to produce all-round physical fitness in his pupils. Under his guidance the pupils, who always exercised naked, learnt how to take care of their bodies by means of a variety of limbering-up exercises and by the application of oil. And indeed, although the *paidotribes* was also responsible for teaching children how to wrestle successfully, how to box and so on, it would be a mistake to see his importance as being an instructor in various athletic or gymnastic skills. His importance from an educational point of view lay in the fact that he taught children how to care for and maintain healthy bodies, just as the *kitharistes* was supposed to teach them to cultivate healthy souls. Central to the classical Athenian ideal was the idea of what a Roman writer was later to refer to as 'a healthy mind in a healthy body' (*mens sana in corpore sano*).

13 *A wrestling match*

THE SCHOOL YEAR

The year was not divided up into terms and holidays. There were no school holidays as such in Athens. But there were a number of religious festivals – in fact Athens had more than any other city – which were national holidays; on these days there was no school. It is probable that for many children the month of February (*Anthesterion*) became in practice one long unofficial holiday. At any rate Theophrastus, who wrote a number of short character sketches of such people as an 'unreasonable man', a 'talkative man' and an 'angry man', has this to say about the 'mean man':

You can bet your life that when he pays back a debt he'll give you four *drachmai* short. When his son is ill and has to miss a few odd days from school he is very careful to subtract the appropriate amount from the teacher's pay. And of course during *Anthesterion* he saves money by not letting his son go to school at all on the few days that are not festival days. [Theophrastus, *Characters* 30]

But then if a great deal of one's education consisted of wrestling naked, covered in olive oil, under the Mediterranean sun, or in washing in a nearby stream, or in singing passages from Homer, perhaps one wouldn't grumble very much about whether there were proper school holidays or not.

Education amongst the poor

The Athenian education was clearly not what we should call a practical or useful education in any immediate sense. It did not help anybody to get a job or to do any particular kind of work. It was concerned to develop the individual, physically and mentally, and to equip him to live a certain kind of life: a gentleman's life. This is not very surprising since the education obviously grew out of the old aristocratic education given to the heroes. But the question arises: what use was all this to the working man? To the farmer's son or the potter's son? Did they have this kind of education?

Many almost certainly did not. Because education never came under the control of the *polis* at Athens, because there was no state system of schools, no *paidonomos* (as there was in Sparta), there was no compulsion on the parents to educate their children in any way. Not surprisingly, the result was, according to Protagoras, that the children of the rich went to school youngest, stayed there longest and left last. In other words many poor parents could neither afford nor perhaps see the point of having their children taught to read and to play the lyre. What good would these things be to a boy who was going to have to scrape his living as a poor farmer? It was not even as if there were any books that one could buy to read.

We know, at any rate, that there were some Athenians who could not even write the names of their leading politicians. For instance, there was the man who attended a meeting in the *agora* at which a vote was being taken to see whether the *strategos* Aristeides, who was known as Aristeides the Just, should be banished from the city. Those who wanted him banished had to write his name down on a broken piece of pottery.

An illiterate rough sort of fellow turned to his neighbour in the crowd, unaware that it was Aristeides himself. He handed him his *ostrakon* (piece of pottery) and asked him to write the name Aristeides for him since he couldn't write. Rather surprised, Aristeides asked the fellow whether Aristeides had ever hurt him. 'No. I don't even know who he is. But I'm sick and tired of hearing everyone call him Just.'

[Plutarch, *Life of Aristeides*]

Perhaps there were few Athenians who could not write at all, but many of the country farmers probably felt pretty shaky in their spelling, like this man in a scene from Aristophanes' play the *Knights*. He is offered a chance to become a leader of the people:

SAUSAGE-SELLER: But look here, my dear chap, I'm not educated at all you know. Well, I mean I know my ABC, at least I know a bit of it.

DEMOSTHENES: Don't worry about that. Quite frankly, it's a pity you know your ABC. To be a leading politician these days it's much better to know absolutely nothing.   [Aristophanes, *Knights* 188ff]

Aristophanes on the traditional education

About half-way through the fifth century there was a minor revolution in the educational practice of the Athenians. Aristophanes later wrote a comedy called the *Clouds* about that revolution. The plot involves a poor old farmer, Strepsiades, and his attempts to get out of paying the debts run up by his aristocratically-inclined playboy son, Pheidippides. Most of these debts are due to Pheidippides' passion for horses – a very proper passion for a gentleman, of course. Strepsiades hopes to save himself by taking advantage of a new type of education that is all the rage in Athens. But first he and his son watch a contest between a representative of the old education and a representative of the new.

Dikaios Logos (The Right point of view) is the representative of the old education; the *Adikos Logos* (The Wrong point of view) of the new. It is not easy to be sure of what Aristophanes' personal attitude to either the old or the new education was. He is too good a satirist to make fun of one side only. But there are reasons for regarding him as being in general rather conservative and opposed to much of the change that rapidly overtook Athenian life in the second half of the fifth century. Certainly, on balance, the *Clouds* seems to ridicule the new trends in education (which will be examined below) more than the old, although Aristophanes rather unfairly makes Socrates the spokesman of these new views. But in this passage it is the traditional education that comes in for a few knocks as the *Dikaios Logos* defends it in terms that can only be interpreted as parody.

DIKAIOS LOGOS: I shall expound the old education as it was pursued when justice and moderation were the aim. First, children were not expected to raise their voices in complaint. They had to march together to the house of the *kitharistes* without making any disturbance, without any extra clothing, even if the snow was piling down. There, standing at attention, they learnt to recite some fine old tune like '*Polis* of hope and glory' or 'Athene, saviour of our land'. The accompaniment to this song, I need hardly add, would be the same tune as that which our fathers used before us. If any boy was so foolish as to try to slip in a new-fangled 'yeah yeah' or 'woe woe', or any of those cacophonous

48

14 *Young man with horse*

harmonies we hear today, he was beaten for being unmusical. Once
they were in the *palaistra* with the *paidotribes*, they sat in orderly
rows so that no passer-by should be shocked by anything he saw. And,
incidentally, when they stood up they smoothed out the sand where
they had been sitting so that the mark of their bottoms would not
encourage any smuttiness. They used oil only above the waist where
it was necessary, and their behaviour in general was modest and decent.

ADIKOS LOGOS: God, this sounds like a description of some pre-
historic society.

DIKAIOS LOGOS: Does it just? Well, you remember, my man, that this
was the education that produced the men who fought and made this
country great, the men of Marathon, the victors against Persia. Just
look what's going on today. Thanks to your approach to life these kids
are so feeble they have to wrap up to keep warm. Pheidippides, my
boy, take my advice, choose an education like your father had. Keep

D   49

15 *A boy being beaten with a sandal*

away from the idle gossip of the *agora* and trivial horseplay at the baths. Avoid this modern tendency to scorn everything. Give up your seat to your elders, show respect to your parents, steer clear of prostitutes and other ladies of doubtful propriety. Hold fast to a sense of modesty; Stand by Respect.

ADIKOS LOGOS: If you listen to one word of this muck – God, what a mummy's darling you'll turn out to be.

DIKAIOS LOGOS: A mummy's boy? A mummy's boy? By God, sir, on the contrary. With this education you'll shine like a bright star in the gymnasium, instead of being the pseudo-intellectual of the *agora*. You, my fine lad, will not be quibbling in a clever-clever manner about some point of law. No. You will compete, crowned with a garland of white reed, with some excellent and loyal friend, in a race along the sand beneath the olive trees – the air hums with happiness and the smell of woodbines is abroad – it is spring – the plane trees rustle lovingly against the elm. Ah, my child, if you do as I say and adopt my attitude you'll grow up with a glistening chest, a clear skin, strong arms, not too talkative, good to look at, good to have. But I warn you. If you forsake the traditions of the past and turn to these new-fangled educational ideas – well, your skin will become pallid and thin; physically you'll be pathetic, haggard and lank; you'll never stop quibbling, proving that black's white and good's bad and day's night and God knows what else. Ugh. Ugh. Ugh. A milksop.

[Aristophanes, *Clouds* 959ff]

The sophists

According to the *Dikaios Logos* the old education, the traditions of his father, are under attack. Worse than that, they seem to face defeat. What, one wonders, has happened? Why have the ideals of modesty and physical health suddenly been left behind?

The years before the Periclean age in Athens were notable for a new spirit of inquiry. All over the Greek world people began to question old assumptions and beliefs, and once such a movement starts it naturally tends to snowball. Why does it rain when it rains? What is happening when it rains? Was Strepsiades right to think that it meant that Zeus was pissing through a sieve? What is an eclipse? How big is the sun? Why is it wrong to eat one's parents? Ought one to obey a king? These and other similar questions began to be asked – and answered. The days were over when one could answer the question 'Why is it right to give up one's seat to an older person?' by saying, 'Because I say so'.

By the middle of the fifth century this movement had begun to leave its mark; many of the old beliefs about the gods, about manners and about customs began to look rather arbitrary, and people therefore took them less seriously. Athens was particularly affected, for Athens was the city of freedom and it was therefore to Athens that the *sophistai* (wise men) naturally came. Sparta, for instance, did not allow foreigners to enter her country and then question her assumptions and beliefs. Free discussion and criticism of the rules would have been out of place there.

One of the problems facing anyone who attempts to write about the 'sophists' is that our evidence for what they were like comes chiefly from a biased source – namely Plato. Writing in the fourth century BC, one of Plato's objectives was to defend the memory of his own teacher, Socrates, who had been put to death for impiety and corrupting the Athenian young in 399 BC. As mentioned above, Aristophanes' play the *Clouds* (produced in 423 BC) had made fun of Socrates, treating him as a hair-splitting and fraudulent nuisance who undermined people's beliefs in the gods and in distinctions between good and bad. Plato's concern was to deny this and to draw a distinction between Socrates who was a sincere seeker after truth and knowledge and the sophists who, by and large, according to Plato, were more concerned to make money and win arguments than to pursue the truth.

What seems indisputable is that whether individual sophists were or were not fools and charlatans, the second half of the fifth century in Athens saw what has been called the birth of an age of rationalism. People were no longer content just to accept the views, the rules and the explanations that had been handed down by their fathers. They wanted to know the reasons why; they wanted to examine and justify opinions for themselves; they wanted evidence for beliefs, and, where no evidence was to be found, they wanted the right to reject those beliefs. This new spirit of inquiry can be seen in most of the written work of the period – in Thucydides' *History*, in the plays of Euripides and in the comedies of Aristophanes himself. And with this spirit of inquiry was born something approaching what we tend to regard as a proper education.

However this new kind of education was never formalised and it did not actually replace the traditional education.

We refer to the sophists as a group, but in point of fact the various sophists who came to Athens did not have anything in common beyond the fact that they were what we should call teachers and charged high fees for lectures. These lectures, which might be on any subject, did not replace the work of the *grammatistes* or the *kitharistes*, for they were on a far higher level. The sophists in fact represent the beginning of higher education. But, because of the high fees, it was only for the sons of the wealthy.

Some were interested in biology, some in politics, some in ethics. Hippias seems to have regarded himself as an expert in everything, if we are to believe what Socrates says to him:

Hippias, I am aware that you are one of the wisest of men in most respects; indeed I have heard you boast as much in the *agora*, telling your audience how much you knew about how many things. I remember you once said, when you were at the Olympic Games, that everything you had with you had been made by you. The ring you wore, you said, was designed and made by you. You had an oil flask, and a strigil for scraping yourself after a bout of wrestling -- you'd made these too, you said. A beautifully woven belt, made by you; poems, made by you -- you were a very good poet, I think you said, and you knew all about music. And I'm quite sure you were expert in many other things, which I'm afraid slip my mind at present. [Plato, *Hippias Minor* 368]

Socrates is obviously poking fun at Hippias, who may well have been a rather conceited fraud. But other sophists were highly intelligent thinkers; for instance there was Protagoras, whose summary of the old education we have already seen. Protagoras' view of the traditional Athenian beliefs -- that they were just custom, without any particular truth in them -- must have offended many old-fashioned Athenians of the *Dikaios Logos* type, but it was none the less important for that. 'Man,' said Protagoras, 'is the measure of all things.' In other words, questions of right and wrong are decided by man, just as man decides what kind of clothes to wear, and they are not, for instance, decided by God. Whether the gods existed or not, Protagoras was not prepared to say; but if they did, he didn't think that they had any direct connection with the world of men.

But the commonest type of sophist was neither the fraud like Hippias nor the genuine philosopher like Protagoras. He was the rhetorician. A *rhetor* is, literally, a public speaker. And at Athens, where political decisions were made at public meetings, where every citizen might expect to have to address the public assembly, where every citizen who went to court had to defend himself, and where, in the absence of most modern forms of entertainment, simply talking in the *agora* or following the subtle arguments of the tragedians were important activities – in such a *polis* the art of public speaking was obviously very important. The orator Demosthenes, for instance, went to the trouble of walking about with pebbles in his mouth in order to cure a stammer.

The rhetoricians, men like Gorgias and Prodicus, offered to teach young men who wanted to succeed in politics to speak well so that they could win popular support for their proposals in the Assembly. The trouble, a serious one, was that in the hands of the more unscrupulous or selfish, this training in successful speech meant a training in skilfully fooling your audience, or, in Aristophanes' phrase, 'making the worse cause appear the better.' It is this kind of education, a training in the knack of cheating your opponent in a debate by clever talking, that the *Adikos Logos* recommends in preference to the traditional education. It is the emphasis on intellectual cleverness and the lack of interest in the old-fashioned outdoor kind of education, that the *Dikaios Logos* regarded as the cause of all the unhealthy, anaemic-looking young men wandering around the *agora*.

Aristophanes on the Higher Education

Aristophanes, while his plays indicate that he himself had been affected by the new spirit of rationalism, none the less makes savage fun of the sophist movement in the *Clouds*. In this passage, for instance, although the *Adikos Logos*, who represents the new thinking, scores some points against his rival, it is difficult to avoid the feeling that Aristophanes' sympathies are not with him.

ADIKOS LOGOS: Very well, then, let's see how sharp your education has made you. Warm baths, you say, are effeminate and to be avoided. But what's wrong with warm baths?

DIKAIOS LOGOS: They make a man feeble.

ADIKOS LOGOS: Feeble, you say. And I suppose you are aware that Hercules, Zeus' own son, has his own warm baths, or have you never heard of the hot springs of Hercules at Thermopylae? And then you criticise these lads who frequent the *agora* in earnest discussion. Have you forgotten that Homer himself praises certain men as *agoretai* (public speakers)? And what about this chastity, this avoidance of sex, that you advise? Think what that means missing: girls, boys, feasting, drinking. Anyway, let's be realistic. It's only human nature to pursue these little pleasures. The point is this: if you slip up, and sooner or

ΑΡΙΣΤΟΦΑΝΗΣ

16 *Aristophanes*

later you will, you're tongue-tied and can't begin to defend yourself. But if you're educated in the new style there's nothing you can't talk your way out of. [Aristophanes, *Clouds* 1036ff]

It is the last remark of the *Adikos Logos* that is crucial. Many Athenians, such as Plato and probably Aristophanes himself, will have welcomed the new spirit of inquiry and the search for knowledge and truth; but what many of them could not welcome was a travesty of this spirit that involved only a new way of seeking power and success without any real regard for truth.

It is difficult to estimate the value of the sophist movement. It might have led to a systematic attempt to redesign the whole of the Athenian system of education, but in fact it did not, largely because Athens herself suffered a crippling blow to her morale when she was defeated by the Spartans in 404 BC at the end of the long and costly Peloponnesian War. And so the activities of the sophists, which involved a radically new idea of what it was to be educated – namely, to be a thinking person – never in fact led to any fundamental change in the educational practice of the Athenians. They continued to pursue the goal of a healthy soul and body and to regard the educated man as one with the habits, tastes and manners of the traditional gentleman. The lectures of the sophists were merely the jam spread on the education of the wealthy few, despite the fact that that jam led to some of the greatest achievements of the Athenian people.

Conclusion

The traditional education at Athens was very similar to the Homeric education out of which it developed. But the system was in some ways a curious hotch potch. Education was supposed to be a matter of private enterprise and yet for some time nobody seemed to show any enterprise: no original ideas came up and standards were not high. The poor were, on the whole, excluded.

There was not supposed to be anything intellectual about this education; that was the gap that the sophists filled. But the most important thing about the Athenian education is that it was not designed, as so much of education is today, to sort people out or to qualify them for particular types of job; it was designed to develop healthy, moderate and sensible people. If we want to mean by *paideia* anything like what we mean by education today, then it was not the schoolmaster who provided it. Ultimately in Athens, no less than in Sparta, 'the *polis* was the true teacher of the man'. The Athenian was really educated simply by the fact that he was a member of that small and tightly-knit community that made the *polis* of Athens. He was educated on the *agora*, on the Pnyx, and in the theatre – and, in the case of a few, by the sophists. For it was in communication with his fellow citizens, in a *polis* that welcomed free thought and the interchange of ideas, that the Athenians learnt to debate, to argue and to think. Above all, it was through the dramas of such men as Sophocles and Euripides, in which fundamental questions about the world and man's place in it were raised and examined, that the Athenian citizen was educated in our sense of the word. Their official education was designed to turn them into sound and healthy citizens; their unofficial education, through the life of the *polis* itself, made them the imaginative and independent-minded people they were.

5

Early Roman education

Mos Maiorum

THE Roman lawyer Cicero, who lived in the troubled times of Julius Caesar, claimed that

The Roman Republic stands strongly on a foundation of men and *mos maiorum* . . . It would have been impossible for men alone, without the support of established customs, to have preserved a state of such widespread power as ours. [Cicero, *Republica* V *1*]

Mos maiorum (ancestral custom) is not an easy phrase to translate, because it meant a great deal more to a Roman than 'ancestral custom' could ever mean to us. What you think of ancestral custom is obviously partly dependent on what you think of your ancestors.

The Romans, at the same time as they overran most of the known world, bringing with them an age of peace and civilisation, remained a very old-fashioned and conservative people. Their new conquests and discoveries, their wealth and power did not change their habits for a long time. The *mos maiorum* included all the religious beliefs, the codes of behaviour, the manners, the rules and even the attitudes that had been known to previous generations. The Roman assumed that the past was to be respected. Cicero evidently feels that the greatness of Rome in his time was founded on the standards of previous generations.

Rome was originally no more than a collection of poor farming families, and she never quite left behind the idea of education as simply a basic training in the *mos maiorum* and the skills necessary for a farmer. The child learnt how to plough the fields and he learnt the Twelve Tables, the main Roman laws.

It is rather as if education today were to involve no more than learning to help one's father run the shop and remembering the Ten Commandments.

17 *Cicero*

PIETAS AND GRAVITAS

The Romans were not an imaginative or quick-witted people. They were very unlike the Athenians. The Athenians admired people who were clever and inventive. The Romans admired reliability, responsibility and duty. The two important things to a Roman were *pietas* and *gravitas*. *Pietas* is a wider term than our 'piety'; it meant devotion not only to the gods but also to the state and to the family. *Gravitas* implies a combination of gravity, dignity and responsibility. The Roman child grew up to think it very important to make the proper sacrifices to the gods, to behave in the manner approved by his fathers and not to make fun of or ridicule the way of life presented to him.

The Roman character

To many people the solemn and conservative Roman character, however admirable it might seem to be in principle, often appears unattractive. None the less, there is something impressive about it.

It is best summed up in the various stories of early Rome which they themselves liked to recall, and in the famous Romans whom they chose to admire. The sense of duty displayed by the farmer Cincinnatus, for instance:

He was working on his small farm by the river Tiber when a deputation sent by the city found him. He was digging a ditch, or something like that. The deputation, after a prayer for God's blessing on him and the country, asked him to put on his toga. He was rather surprised by this; he wondered what was going on, but he told his wife to run to their cottage to get his toga. She did, and he put it on, wiping the sweat away from his face with his arm, and at that moment the deputation greeted him as Dictator of Rome. [Livy, III 27]

This was naturally an extraordinary surprise for the simple peasant Cincinnatus. But he was a Roman, and to him it was clear that his duty was to do whatever he might be called upon to do for the sake of his country. Hundreds of years later, in the time of Christ, the poet Horace was still sounding a similar note: 'It is sweet and noble to die for one's country.' Cincinnatus, by the way, successfully did what was required of him and then, resigning his dictatorship after sixteen days, went back to his farm.

If Cincinnatus was patriotic, Regulus was positively heroic in his unselfish and courageous loyalty to the state:

Regulus was captured by the Carthaginians by a trick. They then sent him back to Rome to tell the Senate to release certain important Carthaginian prisoners. Before he left he swore on oath to the Carthaginians that he would return to them as their prisoner if he could not persuade the Senate to agree to the demand. Now obviously, on the face of it, it was in Regulus' interests to stay in Rome, once he got there, and simply to break his word to the Carthaginians who had captured him. But Regulus was a man of heroism, a man of courage. So what did he do? He walked into that Senate House and actually advised his fellow senators *against* releasing the Carthaginian prisoners. The Senate was persuaded. And then Regulus went back to the Carthaginians, although he knew perfectly well that he would suffer all manner of unspeakable torture. He had to abide by his promise. [Cicero, *De Officiis* III 100]

We may feel that Regulus was brave to the point of stupidity, but it is clear that to the Romans – to Cicero, who tells the story – he was a shining example of patriotism and courage. This was the kind of behaviour approved of by the *mos maiorum*.

PATERFAMILIAS

The first Roman Emperor, Augustus, was one of the most powerful men the world has ever known, and yet he was overcome by the offer of a mere title on one occasion:

Everybody wanted to give him the title of 'Father of the Country'. First the people tried and then the Senate chose Valerius Messala to speak for them. He said: 'Caesar Augustus, it is my privilege to wish you and your family good fortune. The Senate and the Roman people salute you as Father of your country.' At this, tears came to Augustus' eyes and he replied in these words: 'Conscript fathers, now I have achieved my highest ambition.' [Suetonius, *Augustus* 58]

18   *Augustus*

Augustus' reaction may seem very extravagant to us, and no doubt he was exaggerating his gratitude for political reasons, but none the less the title *Pater Patriae* (Father of his Country) would mean a great deal to a Roman.

From earliest times the *pater* (father) had been by far the most important and honoured member of the *familia* (family). To call Augustus *pater patriae* was to suggest that all Italy looked up to him with the mixture of love, awe, admiration and respect, particularly respect, that was due from a family to its head, the *pater*.

The *paterfamilias* (head of the family) at the beginning of Rome's history had complete control, even the power of life and death, over all his family, his wife, children and slaves. And for that reason the Roman in those early days entrusted the upbringing of children to the *paterfamilias* as a matter of course.

CATO

A good example of the type of man that an early Roman *paterfamilias* would have been is provided by Cato, known as Cato the elder to distinguish him from a famous great grandson. In fact Cato lived in the second century BC, late in the history of Republican Rome, but he, like Cicero, was a strong admirer of the good old days and nothing could shake him in his determination to live according to the *mos maiorum*.

Plutarch wrote a life of Cato in which he writes as follows:

By this date the Republic had grown so powerful and widespread that it was proving impossible to maintain the original way of life. New customs, new peoples, new manners were inevitably creeping in. And so, understandably, people admired Cato, because while others became slack and self-indulgent . . . he persevered right to the end and maintained his old-fashioned character. He never wore clothing that cost more than a bare minimum; he drank the same rough wine as the peasants did, even when he was consul; his meat and fish were the cheapest cuts. He was once given a piece of embroidered tapestry, but he sold it because it was too fancy a thing. The walls of his house were rough stone – not even plastered . . . in short, whatever the object might be he reckoned a farthing was too much to spend on it unless it was absolutely necessary.

[Plutarch, *Life of Cato*]

This tough old man, who when a soldier 'drank only water or, if thirsty, water mixed with a little vinegar' once stood for election as censor. The censorship was instituted because, according to the Roman way of thinking, nothing, not even marriage or the upbringing of children, ought to be conducted simply as the fancy took one. Consequently, they used to appoint two men, whom they called censors, to keep an eye on, to steer and, if necessary, to punish anyone who seemed to be getting too lax or to be forgetting the *mos maiorum*.

[Plutarch, *Life of Cato*]

As candidate,

Cato made no attempt to bid for popularity by promising that he would be a lenient censor. On the contrary he made a point of positively guaranteeing his opposition to slack standards. The city was sick, he said. And what it needed was a strict and ruthless doctor.

He was also a good father and an excellent husband. He married a noble but poor wife, because, although he thought that both rich and noble people tended to be supercilious and proud, he was of the opinion that people of noble family would have more sense of shame and would therefore be more dutiful to their husbands in all appropriate matters.

[Plutarch, *Life of Cato*]

Cato was a *paterfamilias* of the early Roman style: honest, upright, a model of *pietas* and *gravitas*. He may also seem to some to have been rigid, hard and unyielding.

Given the importance of the family and the nature of the virtues admired by the Romans, it is hardly surprising that the *paterfamilias* was responsible for his children's education and that he saw the aim of that education as being to produce dutiful citizens.

Education by example

The lawyer Pliny, who lived in the first century AD and who regarded himself as a knowledgeable sort of fellow, has this to say about his ancestors in a letter to a friend:

You know of course that in the past it was the custom of our ancestors to learn from their elders, partly by copying their behaviour and partly by doing as they were instructed. In this way they grew up with a number of firmly-rooted principles of behaviour on which to act, and these principles they, in their turn, taught to their children ... His own father was everyone's teacher, unless he had no father, in which case some family friend was found. Either way they learnt by example and example is the best teacher there is. [Pliny, VIII 14. 4]

Although Pliny talks of the past, the idea of teaching by example and of parental responsibility never died out completely in Rome, even when schools had come into existence. Juvenal, for instance, an embittered poet and satirist of the end of the first century AD, sickened by the selfishness and criminality that he sees all around him, argues that if for no other reason people ought to behave better

so that our behaviour is not imitated by our children. For every one of us is easily influenced when it comes to evil and criminal behaviour . . . So, where there's a father, there should be heard no swearing, there should be seen no disgraceful behaviour . . . You owe it to your children to behave decently . . . Let the thought of them hold you in check. After all, if in the years to come he should do something to enrage the censor, if he should start behaving as evilly as you . . . well, then no doubt you'll be indignant and want to punish him, lose your temper and threaten to throw him out of the house. But, tell me, how are you going to be able to play the part of the stern and righteous *paterfamilias* if your own behaviour is no better? [Juvenal, *Satires* XIV 38ff]

BABIES

The father did not concern himself with the new-born baby; but neither was a slave employed to take over complete control, as often happened in a Greek family. The formation of a child's character began as soon as the baby was born, according to the Romans (and modern psychologists seem to agree), and so

In the good old days no children were entrusted to a hired nurse, but to their own mother's care. That was what a mother was for: to mind the house and watch over the children – and what could be more commendable? As well as the mother, another lady, a relative – responsible and experienced – would have a duty to the children. She had a hand in their lessons, but she also influenced the development of their characters, for in her presence they had to watch what they said, not to mention what they did. For instance Aitia, the mother of the Emperor Augustus, brought him up in this way. And the result we all know: he grew up to be honest, straightforward, honourable and energetic in the pursuit of virtue. [Tacitus, *Dialogues* 28]

The speaker here is a little prejudiced against his own times, and not everyone would agree that Augustus, who signed a warrant for the death of several thousand citizens at the beginning of his career when it seemed necessary, was a model of virtue. But there is no reason to doubt the claim that in the early days of Rome the young child was carefully brought up by the females of the family.

19 *Children playing games*

THE EDUCATION OF CATO'S SON

As one would expect, Cato's son was brought up in the traditional way in the heart of the family:

> Once his son was born, Cato would always be around when his wife washed and dressed him, unless he had urgent matters of state to attend to. His wife, of course, breast-fed her son herself. Later, when he grew older, Cato taught him to read, although as a matter of fact he had a slave who was rather a good grammarian and something of a teacher. But Cato did not feel that it would be appropriate for a slave to ever find himself in the position of reprimanding, or even pulling the ears of, a freeman's son for failing to do his lessons. And besides he did not want to owe anything as important as education to a slave. So he taught his son his grammar, his law and his physical exercises. He showed him how to fight under arms, how to box, how to endure heat and cold and how to swim raging rivers. He also wrote a history book for his son so that he might know something about his ancestors. He never swore in the presence of his son. And so Cato, as if producing a work of art, moulded his son into a virtuous citizen – and with some success. [Plutarch, *Life of Cato*]

With the exception of the history book, all the things that Cato did to educate his son were things normally included in the education of the early Romans.

TOGA VIRILIS

At the age of sixteen a formal ceremony took place in which the boy put on the *toga virilis* (the toga of manhood). He was now a

20 *Scene from the production of a comedy*

citizen and, after a further year spent under the guidance of some
friend of the family, preferably a man in public life, the young man
entered military service. After that his education was complete.
This is how Cicero describes his sixteenth year:

When I had formally put on the *toga virilis* I was taken by my father to the
lawyer Quintus Mucius Scaevola. The idea was that – so far as was
humanly possible – I should never leave the old man's sight. There were
all manner of things that Scaevola used to talk about with intelligence
and penetration. I formed the habit of memorising all his epigrammatic
remarks as a useful addition to my knowledge. [Cicero, *Laelius* 1]

A DIFFERENT VIEW OF EARLY ROMAN EDUCATION

Rather different to the indefatigable Cicero is the character Philolaches in a comedy by Plautus,[1] who wrote at the end of the third
century BC. Philolaches is a playboy who has managed to throw
away a fortune in his father's absence abroad. When he first appears

[1] Although Plautus' plot is taken from a Greek original, his version, played to Roman
audiences, may be taken to reflect Roman attitudes.

on stage he tries to summarise his situation for the benefit of the audience by comparing men to houses.

PHILOLACHES: Right. Now why is a man like a house? Because – first, parents build children. They lay the foundations, and then cause the thing to rise up on its foundations; they guide its growth along the lines as properly laid down on the plans. They're aiming to produce something impressive to look at – something that'll bring credit to them as builders. They spare no expense to turn their children into amazing monuments. They teach them to spell, to speak, to obey the law. They spend all they can – hoping to produce children who'll be the envy of the neighbourhood. It's called keeping up with the Metelli. Then comes the time for military service. Some relative takes over now, and the builder loses sight of his building.

And, sad to relate, in the opinion of Philolaches, this education was a failure:

While they were busy building me – goodness me, I was as fine a Roman as you could hope to meet. A model of *pietas* and *gravitas*. Alas, once it was over and I was on my own, quick as a flash – the whole damned building fell to the ground. [Plautus, *Mostellaria* 183ff]

None the less, it was Romans educated like this who turned a village of shepherds into the capital of the world.

6

Rome captures Greece and Greece captures Rome

PHILOLACHES saw himself as a building that fell down as soon as the guiding hand of the parents who 'built him up' was removed. But the essence of the old Roman education did not disintegrate so quickly. We have already seen latter-day Romans such as Cicero and Pliny display considerable respect for the past, and much of the old educational ways survived into the imperial period of Rome. But there were changes, and a great many of them followed on Rome's conquest of Greece.

For, although it was the Roman legions that finally defeated the Greek cities (which were by now pale shadows of their former glorious selves) in battle (146 BC), the truth, as Horace said, was that:

Greece, once captured, took hold of her crude conqueror and brought sophistication to uneducated Latium ... although the signs of our country background lived on for a while, indeed still live on. It was only recently that the Roman turned his mind to a study of Greek literature. [Horace, *Epistles* II 1.56]

But it was not only Greek literature that the Romans gradually began to take over from their defeated enemy. They also taught their children to speak Greek; they even imitated the Greek system of education. Gone were the good old days:

Nowadays we hand our new-born babies over to a Greek slave girl – sometimes she's given a helping hand by a male slave, a rogue, good for nothing as likely as not. So our children grow up listening to the fairy tales of such poor teachers as these. There's absolutely no attempt these days for anyone to set a good example in front of the children. Parents don't bother to bring up their children properly according to the *mos maiorum* anymore – and as a result our children have no *gravitas*, no *pietas*. [Tacitus, *Dialogus* 29]

21　*Stages in the upbringing of a Roman boy*

We have met this speaker before and noted his tendency to exaggerate. However, as Rome developed from her humble beginnings to become conqueror of the world, many parents ceased to regard the education of their children as of great importance.

THE NEW ROMAN VALUES

As Rome grew in size and power after the Punic Wars, the family ceased to be so tightly-knit a unit, and it ceased to be so important. In addition the growth of a vast dependent empire brought in a completely new way of life, and some new values.

Juvenal disliked most of them. In furious scorn he exclaimed:

Then let money be Lord of all. Let the magistrate step aside for the slave – provided the slave has grown rich. We worship no god as fervently as we worship Wealth – even if, wretched Cash, you do not yet have your own private temple. [Juvenal, *Satires* I 112ff]

A new commercial streak had arisen in the new Rome; a new town-life replaced the old country ways; and the *mos maiorum* was no longer universally and automatically admired.

Greek influence

It is impossible to be certain when the Greek influence first began to make itself felt and when the first schools were set up in Rome. But since the system of school education superficially resembles that of the Greeks it is probable that the two developments coincided.

The historian Livy, who wrote in the time of the Emperor Augustus, refers to a school as in existence at a very early date. He tells us this story which must be dated to about 450 BC, that is to say to the time when Pericles came into prominence in Athens and when Rome was still an unheard-of backwater.

One morning Verginia was seized as she entered the forum to go to school. She was a girl of poor parents, but at the same time she was very beautiful. The man who had grabbed her told her to follow him, threatening that he'd drag her by force if she refused to come quietly. The girl was terrified, but her nurse shouted for help and at once a number of people gathered round. [Livy, III 44]

The forum, being the heart of the city, is admittedly exactly where one expects a school to be. It was in the forum that the lawyers, businessmen, magistrates and even the simple shoppers or loafers conducted a large part of their business. It was the centre of Roman life: important temples were built here, and here the people assembled for any official voting. But few historians will accept that there can have been a school there at such an early date. In 450 the *mos maiorum* still held sway and education was still in the hands of the *paterfamilias*.

We know, however, that by Cato's time the influence of Greece was so strong that when some famous Greek teachers arrived in Rome on official business the old-fashioned Cato was immediately very worried:

All the bright young men had gone at once to meet these visiting Greek sophists ... and they were so impressed that they soon lost all interest in everything except the pursuit of knowledge. On the whole, Roman public opinion approved of this. Cato however was extremely suspicious of this interest in words and literature, and he was afraid that everyone would become so fond of discussing what to do that they'd soon stop actually doing anything. He decided to try and get rid of the Greeks, and so he went to the Senate and argued that the visitors should be given whatever they had come for. Then, he said, they can go home and talk to their own children in their own schools, leaving the Roman youth to obey our laws and our teachers. [Plutarch, *Life of Cato*]

But Cato was fighting a losing battle. Once the idea of schools and literature as a part of education had been taken over from the Greeks it was impossible to keep the study of Greek literature out of the schools. For one simple reason: the Romans at this early date had virtually no literature of their own.

A near contemporary of Cato made a much better job of adapting to new circumstances:

Aemilius Paulus devoted himself to the education of his children. He brought them up both as he himself had been brought up, according to the *mos maiorum*, and also in the Greek manner. He was very keen on the Greek methods and therefore hired masters to teach them grammar, logic and rhetoric, as well as teachers of drawing, hunting and athletics.

[Plutarch, *Life of Aemilius*]

MUSIC

Although Roman education was now to become completely infected by Greek education, there were none the less two important features of the latter which never really caught on in the Roman world. They were music and athletics. To the Greeks, as we have seen, music was an essential part of civilised life: *mousike* could be used as a synonym for *paideia*. A man who could neither sing nor play the lyre was uncouth and boorish. He was uneducated. But the Romans never felt this way.

The emperor Nero, for instance, was certainly not respected in any way for his undoubtedly genuine interest in, and even talent for music. Whether he really played the fiddle while Rome burned will perhaps never be known for certain. But it seems clear that he took his singing so seriously that

He would lie down with a large slab of lead placed on his chest, make himself sick in order to keep himself thin, and refuse to eat apples because they were thought to be bad for the vocal chords. In actual fact he had a pathetic voice, but he thought he was good enough to make public performances. Nobody was allowed to leave the theatre while he was performing, and so women had to give birth to children in the theatre and some people were so bored that they pretended to be dead so that they would be carried out for burial . . . None the less his Roman audiences did not satisfy him so he decided to make a tour of Greece: 'The Greeks alone are worthy of my genius,' he said. 'They understand music.'

[Suetonius, *Nero* 20–23]

To the Romans of the old stamp, music was almost indecent. Cato, trying to abuse a man as roughly as he could, finally remarked 'and furthermore he sings'. But even at the end of the Republic the historian Sallust could use music as a sign of indecency in his description of Sempronia, a woman of decidedly dubious reputation:

This woman had more than once committed crimes that would make a modest man blush. She was in fact a very lucky woman: well-born, good-looking, with a fine husband and children. She was also well-educated in Greek and Roman literature, and as well as having many other talents which added to her attraction she could play the lyre and dance rather more skilfully than any decent woman need. [Sallust, *Catiline* XXV 2]

However there seems little doubt that music on a popular level could be a money-making business. The poet Martial, for instance, strikes a very modern note when he suggests that all this education business is really a waste of time. If you want your child to get on in life, don't bother about school – let him join a pop group:

For a long time, Lupus, you have been anxiously asking me what teacher you ought to get your son. My advice is not to waste your time with the standard teacher of grammar or rhetoric; and don't make the boy study the great works of literature. Cicero can look after himself, without our having to read him. If your son is inclined to be artistic – cut him off, throw him out. But now, suppose he's interested in making money – then teach him to be a harp or flute player. By the way, if he's really stupid, he'd better be an engineer. [Martial, V 56]

The Romans did take over a part of what the Greeks meant by *mousike*, because they took over the literature of the Greeks. But whereas the Greeks treated such works as the poems of Homer primarily as works to be recited or sung and enjoyed, the Romans treated them as works to be studied. They shared neither the Greek view that singing and playing musical instruments were marks of the educated man nor the view that through *mousike* the soul or inner nature of man became moderate and cultivated.

ATHLETICS

Similarly the Romans did not share the Greek view that a healthy and athletic body was an end in itself. Although the Greeks had other reasons too for concentrating on gymnastics (for instance, their love of competition), one of their reasons had always been simply their feeling that healthy and beautiful bodies were attractive: beauty of any kind was an end in itself to most Greeks. The Romans exercised too, but with less enthusiasm, and as a means to the end of being able to carry out the duties of life, such as serving as a soldier on campaign. Cato, as we have seen, taught his sons to swim raging

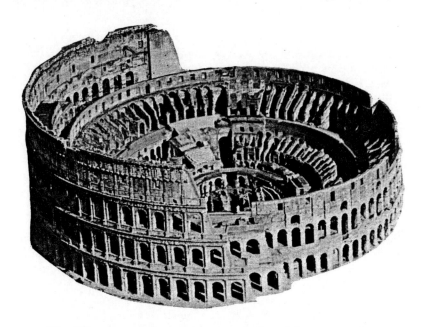

22   *The Colosseum: scene of many great gladiatorial contests and games*

rivers, but he did this so that they would be tougher, not for any interest in swimming itself.

Whereas Greeks would assemble together in the *palaistra* to compete, the Romans would assemble to watch other people compete: gladiators and charioteers. The Greeks were a nation of amateur sportsmen, the Romans of professional punters. Scipio Africanus was actually accused of being unroman on the grounds that

his clothes and the way he walked were not Roman. He used to walk about the gymnasium dressed in the Greek manner, and then he used to waste his time with literature and athletics ... He seemed to have forgotten all about the enemy, Carthage. The army was completely undisciplined. In fact it was more of a danger to Rome than Carthage.
[Livy, XXIX 19]

It is clear, then, that there were certain important differences between Greek education and the Graeco-Roman education that developed in the Roman world after 146 BC. None the less the influence of Greece was considerable, as we shall see in the next chapter.

7

Graeco-Roman education

Responsibility for education

THERE were three stages of education under the developed Graeco-Roman system. At the age of seven the child went to the *litterator*, who was the equivalent of the Greek *grammatistes*; then he went to the *grammaticus* who was similar to the *kitharistes* in some respects, and finally to the *rhetor* who was closely modelled on the *sophist*.

But not everyone went to school. There was no law demanding it, for education was still regarded as essentially the concern of the parents, even if they seldom undertook the teaching themselves any more. As Cicero said,

It has never been the Roman practice to have some definite system of education fixed by law for the children of freemen, nor even to have one officially recognised; it has never been our practice to have a uniform system at all. [Cicero, *Respublica* IV 3.3]

All that can be said is that it was up to parents to see to the education of their children.

THE PARENTS

Needless to say there were many different kinds of parent to be found then as now. There is a letter from Pliny to a friend in which he advises the friend to send his son to the school of a *rhetor*:

He will only turn out to be a worthy son of his father and grandfather if he is educated from the beginning along the proper lines. Because of his youth you have kept him at home up to now and had teachers come to him there. But now the time has come to tackle something more demanding. We must find a school of rhetoric where, as well as getting good rhetorical training, he will be kept up to the mark in his manners and his morals. He's a good-looking boy and therefore, I think, will need to be protected from unwanted advances. We need a scholar, a guardian and a noble example rolled into one. [Pliny, III 3.3]

It doesn't sound as if the child in question is going to be given much opportunity to relax and enjoy himself, but he is at least fortunate in that he seems to be in the hands of people of some sense. Pliny may sound rather pompous and solemn at times, but he is preferable as a guardian to the self-made know-it-all whom we meet in Petronius' *Satyricon*. The scene is a dinner party given by the wealthy freedman Trimalchio. One of his fellow freedmen begins to get rather hostile to some of his more well-bred guests; finally he turns on his neighbour:

Look here, you sheep's head, quit your laughing, can't you? Why do you keep laughing down your nose at all Trimalchio's knick-knacks and such? No doubt you're richer and used to finer things, eh? I'm not easily annoyed, by God – but, by God I'm angry now. When I've finished with you and your grinnery face – Why, just because you're a Roman knight – All right, so I didn't learn geometry, didn't do essay-writing and such rubbish. But I can read; I can count. And I'll bet that did me more good than the money your father wasted on your schol-la-dee-da fees with the rhetorician. There's more ways of skinning a dog than three, you know. I was taught by a real teacher: 'Hold on to what you've got and mind how you go,' said he. That's what I call education. That's what made me what I am today.' [Petronius, *Satyricon* 57]

School

The schoolroom was generally nothing more than a simple room hired by the teacher, perhaps at the back of some shop in the forum. It might be cut off from the bustle outside by a curtain. We know this because the two words used to describe the early schools, *taberna* and *pergula*, in fact both mean 'shopkeepers' booth'. Later the word *ludus*, which originally meant diversion or pastime, became the usual word for an elementary school, and *schola* (from the Greek *schole* meaning leisure) for the secondary school.

The pupils sat on wooden stools, while the master sat on a high-backed chair known as a *cathedra* (from which we get the expression 'to speak *ex cathedra*' meaning 'with authority'). The room might be enlivened with the busts of famous men – yet another sign of the Roman love of setting examples before children.

74

23 *A scene in the school-room*

THE TEACHERS

The man who was in charge of this gloomy hole in the wall, the teacher, was, as always, badly paid. This is yet another thought to send Juvenal off in fury:

And whoever paid such teachers as the grammarians Celadus and Palaemon a half of what they deserve? But although the wage of the *grammaticus* is minute – and good heavens, it's even less than the *rhetor* gets which isn't saying much – everybody else you can imagine wants a slice of it: the pupil's *paidagogos*, the pupil himself, for God's sake. But I advise you, friend teacher, accept this loss of half your pittance – thank God that you've got even that half in return for sitting from early dawn in a cell that no tradesman, no workman, would tolerate. Be thankful, I say, that you earned as much as a halfpenny for your grimy labours.

And, as if being cheated wasn't enough, the poor wretch of a teacher has to put up with the insufferable demands of parents. He has to be word-perfect in his grammar, he has to be able to quote every date accurately, and to answer every question, however obscure, that his pupils may put to him at any place at any time – however inconvenient.

[Juvenal, *Satires* VII 215ff]

If teachers were generally as badly-paid and as badly-treated as Juvenal suggests, it is not perhaps surprising that some of them became rather harsh, and hence unpopular. There are many references to beatings; Horace's schoolmaster was known as Orbilius the Beater. And Martial even wrote an Ode to the Cane:

We are the fennel wood originally brought to earth by Prometheus. To boys we are unbearable – to teachers unbeatable. [Martial, XIV 80]

Needless to say, not all teachers were cruel tyrants; there were some people who thought that parents ought to be condemned for the way in which they interfered with the teacher and prevented him punishing children; and Horace refers to 'teachers giving sweets to children to bribe then into learning their ABC'.

But on balance we can well believe Pliny when he says that

a good deal of persuasion, as well as some financial incentive, is needed to get anyone to choose to put up with the boredom and hard work involved in teaching children. [Pliny, I 8.11]

THE SCHOOL DAY BEGINS

The school day started early, as we have already seen from Juvenal's reference to the impoverished teacher in his cell-like room before dawn. Boys and girls went off together, accompanied, if they came from a wealthy town family, by a *paedagogus*. Thus Horace was proud and grateful to his father for moving to Rome and devoting something of his savings to his son's education:

If – forgive me talking about myself in this way – if I am a decent upright sort of fellow, and if I have some good friends – well, all this is thanks to my father. He was a poor farmer but he wouldn't send me to the local school, even though all the children of the local gentry used to go there, carrying their satchels and slates, not to mention the paltry trifle taken once a month as pay for the teacher. No, he took me to Rome. A bold decision for a poor man to make. And there he had me taught the sort of thing a senator's son would be taught. And so I went through the street accompanied by a *paedogogus*, and benefited from excellent teachers – including my own father. [Horace, *Satires*, I 6.69]

In other words Horace felt that he benefited from schooling in Rome just as a boy today might feel that he had benefited if his parents could afford to give him a good public school education.

The early start and the sound of many children making their way to school before cock-crow did not please everybody. It did not please Martial, for a start:

Damn you, you contemptible schoolmaster, the epitome of all that boys and girls can't stand. By God, the cocks aren't crowing yet, and there you are – roaring and whacking away. Smack, thwack – it's like the sound of a metal-beater; it's louder than the roar at the Circus for the favourite chariot. We don't ask for everything – we don't expect a full night's sleep. A little insomnia never harmed anyone. But a little sleep never did either. Dismiss your school. Look, you talkative old bore, I'll pay you what you earn to teach if you'll just shut up. [Martial, IX 68]

THE PAEDAGOGUS

The *paedagogus* is of course, as his name reveals, a direct imitation of the Greek attendant. The Roman *paedagogus* almost certainly had less opportunity to influence the child than his Greek counterpart; on the other hand, since he was generally a Greek slave he did have the specific job of teaching Greek. It still seemed reasonable to hold the *paedagogus* responsible for the behaviour of his charge as this scene from Plautus' *Mostellaria* shows. Tranio, who is Philolaches' *paedagogus*, is being severely criticised by a fellow slave:

You'd better make hay while the sun shines, Tranio. Eat, drink and be merry – spend the master's cash and ruin the master's spendthrift son. Rave the night away in true Greek style while you can, matey. Do you think the master wanted you to look after his son like this? There was a time when the master's son was known for his decency and respectability. Now he's a regular scoundrel, and all thanks to your teaching.

[Plautus, *Mostellaria* 20ff]

A SCHOOL EXERCISE: MY DAY

Incredible as it may seem, we still possess a copy of an essay written by a Roman schoolboy in about AD 200. The essay is an account of the boy's school day, and the following is a short extract from it:

As soon as it's dawn I summon the slave and get him to open the window. It's cold – too cold to put my feet on the tiles – so I sit on my bed till the slave has passed me my shoes and stockings. Then, when water has been brought, I wash. Then I rub my teeth, spit, and blow my nose, as people do.

I go and say good morning to my parents with my *paedogogus* and nurse, and then set off for school. The *paedogogus* comes with me, of course, and another slave carries my slate.

I meet up with some of my schoolfriends outside the schoolroom. Then I climb the stairs, smooth down my hair and enter the room, saying good morning to the teacher.

He stays at school until it is time for a lunch break of olives, cheese and bread, which he has at home, and then he returns for the afternoon lessons. The day ends with a visit to the baths.

Teacher: have pity on your little ones. Then perhaps the little curly-headed ones will pay attention, perhaps they will even love their arithmetic teacher – a little . . . It is July, the sun is ablaze and the fields are yellow with ripe corn . . . Put away the cane, the sign of the *paedogogus*, and let it rest until October. [Martial, X 62]

This little poem of Martial makes it fairly clear that Roman children were no better off than Greek children when it came to holidays. The poet is evidently asking the teacher to let the children go as a special dispensation; we may therefore conclude that there was not normally an official summer holiday.

However, as in Greece, any festival day was automatically a school holiday. In addition, market days (*nundinae*) and any days on which there was some public spectacle, such as a triumph or a gladiatoral show, would almost certainly have closed the schools.

The *litterator*

The *litterator* (also known as the *magister ludi* or *primus magister*) taught reading and writing and he was helped by the *calculator* who taught simple arithmetic. Horace was critical of this part of his education and suggested that a preoccupation with figures was responsible for making the Romans less artistic than the Greeks:

The Muse gave the Greeks a sharp mind and a clever tongue: their reward was recognition. The Roman boys learn, with a great deal of calculation, to divide one penny by a hundred. 'Very well, son of Albinus: what do you get if you take five-twelfths away from an ounce? Come on, come on. Quick, child.' 'A third.' 'Good. Nobody'll be able to pull a fast one on you. Add one ounce then. What do you get?' 'A half.' Is it any wonder that, after making our children go through this sort of thing, this petty interest in cash, none of them become poets?

[Horace, *Ars Poetica* 323ff]

'One and one equals two,' sang St Augustine, 'two plus two equals four – oh, how I hated that chant.'

Letters were learnt by the same copying process that the Greek *grammatistes* had employed. Then, when the child could write well enough to read complete sentences, he would be made to copy out

24 *Roman writing materials*

useful phrases, such as *'laborare est orare'* (to work is to pray), and these he would then learn.

The years spent with the *litterator* and *calculator* are roughly equivalent to the time spent in primary school under our system, but few primary schools today could be as rigid as the Roman system seems to have been. It is said sometimes that young children like to be organised and told what to do: if that is true, the Roman schoolboy must have been very happy with the *litterator*. Here is another extract from the schoolboy's essay already quoted; he is describing the copying lesson:

I copy the letters and then show the work to the teacher. He corrects it and copies it out properly. I get ready to start again by rubbing the wax smooth – that's a job, the wax is too hard. Here we go: ink and papyrus now. Up ... and down ... up and down ... and then along comes teacher and says I deserve to be whipped.

The *grammaticus*

The *grammaticus* was no more respected than the *litterator*. We have already learnt from Juvenal that parents expected him to be the fount of all wisdom – yet gave him no thanks for it. His job was to teach Latin and Greek literature. The children had to recite passages from the chosen authors and to write commentaries on them. Until the very end of the first century BC there had not really been any Roman authors to read, but by the beginning of the imperial period the works of Virgil, Cicero, Sallust and Terence had become standard school works, rather like Shakespeare has become in our schools. Horace, who himself later became a standard author in schools, recalls his own school days when, for lack of any other poetry, he had been made to study the work of someone called Livius:

Popular taste is by no means a reliable guide. For instance there is a fashion that admires the poets of long ago and argues that great art is no longer being produced – a foolish fashion. Don't think that I'm ridiculing Livius' poems – far be it from me to ridicule verses which my old *grammaticus* Orbilius the Beater dictated to me as a boy. But to suggest that Livius' poems are without fault or that they are beautiful – well that would be frankly absurd. [Horace, *Epistles* II 1.63ff]

But even with the arrival of genuine works of art in their own right, such as Virgil's *Aeneid* and Horace's own poetry, the Romans were not quite in a position to successfully copy the Greeks. Greek children learnt the poems of Homer and others from the *grammatistes* and *kitharistes*, but when they did this, as we saw, they were learning something central to their own civilisation and culture. They were not learning Good Poetry – at least, that was not the way they saw it – they were hearing glorious accounts of their own past, stirring examples of how to behave; they were simply and unselfconsciously acquainting themselves with their heritage.

But why did the Romans learn Greek? And why did they study their own poetry, so much of which was consciously taken over from or modelled on Greek originals? Part of the answer may well be that it had become the smart thing to do. But there was more to it than that. The Greeks had built up a body of works in most spheres of inquiry and interest: drama, philosophy, poetry, medicine and science, for example. The Romans were implicitly paying tribute to the achievements of the Greeks and at the same time using the material that they studied as a basis from which to develop their own intellectual inquiries.

None the less, in terms of education a great deal of what went on must have seemed sterile and irrelevant to many Roman children. The *grammaticus* asked his pupils questions such as, 'How many verbs are there in this poem? How many nouns?' These questions may have their place, but they do not belong in the original Greek idea of studying literature. Still less did the Romans' concern with classifying different kinds of adjective or different kinds of literary fault have its origins in the traditional Greek education. However, these philological exercises did have *a* Greek origin, which perhaps explains why the Romans introduced them into their schools, for the science of philology had originated with Greeks such as Dionysius Thrax who lived and worked in Rhodes during the second half of the second century BC.

The lessons of the philological exercises were put to good use when the children, having first of all listened to the *grammaticus* reading through a passage and explaining it (*praelectio*), had afterwards read the passage aloud themselves. For then they were expected to offer critical comments on the passage, relating both to its style or form and to its content. They were also required to learn a number of passages by heart. And here it should perhaps be stressed that in a culture that has relatively little printed material and where what there is of it is expensive and hard to come by, it is obviously of considerable importance to develop one's memory. Much of the Roman educational pattern, which at times seems monotonous to us, can be defended on the grounds that it was intended to develop the memory that is essential in an oral culture.

The purpose of the *grammaticus'* teaching, then, was to give his pupils a knowledge of the 'classics', as they already were, and to teach them to speak Greek, which had become the second language of the Roman Empire, because the Greeks were the only truly civilised people whom the Romans conquered.

As far as the Roman was concerned, the essential point of

translating Greek into Latin, and vice versa, is that it is a useful exercise for developing one's precision with words ... and, of course, working with the best models does tend to improve one's own literary style.

[Pliny, VII 9]

The *rhetor*

According to the old-fashioned speaker in Tacitus' *Dialogue on oratory*, the *litterator* and *grammaticus* are not very effective teachers anyway:

Not nearly enough work is done on literature and history ... Everybody makes a bee-line for the so-called rhetorician.

The *rhetor* (teacher of eloquence) was a direct imitation of the *sophistes*, and we have already seen some of the staid Romans such as Cato objected to the outbreak of the new educational style imported from Greece. In the past, Romans had learnt the art of public speaking by example. With their fathers they stood in the forum or in the senate house and heard the speeches of the great orators. But now the art of oratory (i.e. fluency of speech and cogency of argument) could be picked up in the schoolroom. There were certain fixed conventions or rules for orators, just as there are fixed conventions for barristers' speeches today, and these rules were picked up by the student from his study of preparatory exercises which were really just examples of model speeches. Then the pupil himself was expected to compose imaginary speeches and to deliver them to an audience consisting of his fellow students. An important part of this exercise (*declamatio*) was that the speaker should deliver his speech with appropriate facial gestures and movements of his hands.

There were two different kinds of *declamatio*. In one case (*suasoria*) the exercise consisted of attempting to produce an imaginary speech justifying some course of action, historical or fictional. There are many examples of the *suasoria* referred to by Roman writers, such as, 'Should Sulla have resigned his dictatorship?' 'Should Cato have committed suicide?' and 'Should Alexander have crossed the Ocean?'. Clearly, apart from the fact that the *suasoria* had to be delivered as a speech, this exercise is not all that different from the setting of certain types of essay in schools today. And, then, as now, this procedure had its critics. Juvenal, for instance, satirises the business when he puts these words into the mouth of the *rhetor*:

'Why should I pay you? What have I learnt from you?' asks the student. According to him it is my fault that he feels no stirring of the heart as he drones on about dread Hannibal regularly once a week, asking if Hannibal should have made straight for the city from Cannae or led his soldiers on in the rain. [Juvenal, *Satires* VII 158ff]

The other kind of *declamatio*, the *controversia*, consisted of an attempt to argue for or against a specific legal case. For example, 'Suppose that the law states that if a woman has been seduced she can choose either to have her seducer condemned to death or to marry him without giving him any dowry. A man seduces two women on the same night. One asks for him to be put to death, the other chooses to marry him. Defend either proposal.'

Such exercises could of course involve considerable ingenuity on the part of the *rhetor* or his students. An opportunity was provided both to construct sound arguments and to make telling points by means of a neat turn of phrase, a stroke of wit or a clever epigram. Furthermore, in a culture that was still predominantly oral there was some practical point in cultivating the art of speech – the more so since the law courts and politics, where such skills would be of particular use, remained for a long time the natural places for any aspiring young man to seek to make his mark.

But from about the time of Augustus' principate the art of *declamatio* gradually became divorced from these utilitarian considerations, changed its nature, and, in the eyes of many Roman and modern critics, thereby became an artificial and rather deplorable exercise. As the political situation changed, with the emperors becoming more autocratic, so that there was less opportunity for advocates in the courts and would-be politicians to really speak their minds, the art of *declamatio* grew away from its supposed practical point. Practitioners began to defend it on its own terms as a form of artistic expression, rather like ballet or opera. This in turn brought about a tendency for *rhetors* and their students to take up totally unreal and improbable themes to dilate on. And that finally led to a situation in which all the emphasis fell on the manner of presentation rather than the content. Whereas in the early days a student was expected to offer a convincing argument, as time progressed, the concern became more and more simply to be original and to gain applause for subtlety and extravagance, regardless of the relevance to the argument of what was said.

It was with these sort of considerations in mind that Petronius, writing in the time of Nero, opened his *Satyricon* with this blast against rhetoricians:

I take the view that the schools of the *rhetors* make idiots of our young men, because they offer nothing that relates to real life. It's all pirates standing in chains on the beach, tyrants ordering sons to cut their fathers' heads off, oracles demanding the blood of three virgins, and so on. Improbable fairy stories to argue around – and the manner of speech demanded is a ludicrous amalgamation of honeyed words and delicate phrases that fit ill with the bloody subject-matter. [Petronius, *Satyricon* 1]

And Tacitus too voiced the same complaint: 'The real orator is one who speaks with a convincing nobility and brilliance, while at the same time doing justice to his subject.' That was the belief of the great Roman orators of the past such as Cicero, he argues, and they

83

regarded an untiring journey through every branch of learning as a necessary preliminary to speechifying. They understood that what was needed:

was not to practise exercises in the school of rhetoric, not simply to train the voice and tonal inflections with imaginary disputes bearing no relation to reality, but to study the nature of virtue and vice, justice and injustice.
[Tacitus, *Diàlogus* '31]

The art of the *rhetor*, closely modelled on that of the sophist, evidently suffered a severe decline. Many of the Greek sophists may have been frauds, arguing for the sake of arguing and winning, or for the sake of money. Certainly Aristophanes had made such a charge against them. But at least even the worst of them may have managed to evoke a genuine enthusiasm in their pupils, for they were not caught up in the stranglehold of fixed ideas about the presentation of an argument as a minor art form. The result, by and large, was that the Athenians were really moved by a spirit of inquiry and a desire to question and argue. They wanted to find out the truth. They cared. Debate and public speaking were seen as means to the end of clarifying issues and problems.

The same was no doubt true of the Romans at first. Cicero, for all his artifice and subtle but suspect argumentation, had a real concern for the substance or content of what he was saying. But gradually a change came about, and debating became something to pursue solely for the purpose of improving debating technique.

It is perhaps hardly surprising that in most people's eyes the *rhetor* did not stand much higher than his junior colleagues in the teaching profession, as this final quotation from the letters of Pliny reveals:

Has the news reached you? Valerius Licinianus has taken up teaching rhetoric in Sicily. What a fall. What a drop. Only yesterday he was a senator and an orator – now an exile and a *rhetor*. At his first lecture he came in dressed in a Greek cloak and announced that he would dilate on this theme: 'How the mighty are fallen.' [Pliny, IV. 11]

Conclusion

To conservatives such as Tacitus and Cato the way in which education developed in the Roman world was just a long story of decline. We may perhaps judge the matter slightly differently, seeing the

25　*A stern teacher and a pupil*

period towards the end of the Republic as a highspot. That was the time when Rome, a little uneasily at first, tried to take over something of the Athenian ideal.

Early Roman education had concentrated on turning children into virtuous adults with a proper respect for the Roman way of life. From our point of view such a view of education seems both narrow and lacking in any concern for independent thought or critical opinion. With the introduction of the study of literature, at first Greek and then Roman, and with the introduction of the schools of rhetoric, there begins a system of education that attempts to learn from the best of the past and to encourage pupils to think for themselves in a lucid and coherent manner. This was the education that helped to produce Rome's own genius in the poetry of Virgil and Horace, in the legal and philosophical writings of Cicero, and in the histories of Tacitus.

It was only in later years, as the tyrannical nature of the principate closed up avenues for the individual's free expression, that this system began to lose its vitality and became merely a shadow of itself: a thing without substance, mere appearance.

Epilogue

To understand the educational system of a people is to be half-way towards understanding them. In the aristocratic education of Homer's heroes we see the beginning of that competitive spirit, that love of glory and that freedom that never entirely left the Greeks. In Athens we see a more developed form in which a degree of a sense of community spirit has been added, and ultimately an intellectual interest. The Greeks on the whole, and the fifth-century Athenians in particular, were an excited, open and cheerful people at their best. Their aim in education was not to qualify for something beyond education; it was rather to shape the human body and soul in the process of education.

The Spartans set themselves a special task: the preservation of the status quo – unity rather than individuality, courage rather than initiative. In the modern world the totalitarian regimes seem in many ways to be taking a leaf from the Spartan book. We should be foolish to underestimate what can be achieved by such single-minded devotion to an educational ideal.

Finally, there are the Romans. In the beginning they were a formidable and impressive people, even if somewhat dull and unattractive. And then came the attempt to slip into the Greek skin: to be what they were not. For a time, it was not without its merits, but in the end it failed: it produced the artificial education *par excellence*.

But there is something else, besides an understanding of the Greeks and Romans, that can be gained from a study of their educational systems – and that is a number of ideas, possibly even some lessons. Throughout this book I have had occasion to refer to the ideal of producing critical thinking or of an education designed to encourage people to think for themselves. This ideal is a common one amongst educationalists in our society today, even if it does not always seem that the ideal is effectively being put into practice. Nor is it surprising that it should be our ideal, for it goes hand in hand with the ideal of democracy in which (in theory) each man shall speak for himself.

Similarly, it is not surprising that the impact of the sophists and their desire to question was first felt in democratic Athens. Because we have this ideal, for the most part, we are in the fortunate position of feeling free to consider the relative merits of different educational ideals – including our own. We can, if we choose, freely discuss whether education should ideally lead people to freely discuss such questions.

From the Greeks and Romans we can extract such totally different ideals as the view that education involves inculcating in people the style of life of the society, that it involves giving children skills that are suitable to the nature of society, that it involves introducing children to certain conventional interests, that it involves studying literature, that it involves physical health as well as mental health, that it involves learning to debate with skill, that it involves learning to question, and so on. The suggestions that can be found amongst the Greeks and Romans bear a marked resemblance to suggestions that are still being put forward today.

Index